One Test After Another

Also by Henry Blofeld
Caught Short of the Boundary

One Test After Another

Life in International Cricket

HENRY BLOFELD

STANLEY PAUL
London Melbourne Sydney Auckland Johannesburg

For Suki and Anna with love

Stanley Paul & Co. Ltd
An imprint of Century-Hutchinson Publishing Co. Ltd

17–21 Conway Street, London W1P 6JD

Hutchinson Group (Australia) Pty Ltd
16–22 Church Street, Hawthorn, Melbourne, Victoria 3122

Hutchinson Group (NZ) Ltd
32–34 View Road, PO Box 40–086, Glenfield, Auckland 10

Hutchinson Group (SA) Pty Ltd
PO Box 337, Bergvlei 2012, South Africa

First published 1985
© Henry Blofeld 1985

Set in 11/13pt Monophoto Sabon

Printed and bound in Great Britain by Butler & Tanner Ltd, Frome and London

British Cataloguing in Publication Data
Blofeld, Henry
    One test after another: life in international
    cricket
    1. Test matches (Cricket)
    I. Title
    796.35′865′0924   GV923

ISBN 0 09 162290 5

Contents

1   The Rise of World Series Cricket   7
2   Consequences   16
3   The Lure of the West Indies   23
4   A New Season   33
5   On Board the Cricket Caravan   44
6   Cricket and Other Distractions   53
7   Farewell Test   57
8   Three Remarkable Australians   64
9   The One-Day Yo-Yo   74
10   A First Victory for Pakistan   79
11   Allegations and an Auto-Rickshaw Ride   88
12   And So To Faisalabad   99
13   Sarfraz versus Botham   112
14   Hunting Wild Boar   126
15   Relaxing on Rhodes   138
16   The Mixture as Before   142
17   Further Adventures   161

1
The Rise of World Series Cricket

Cricket in Australia has been an intriguing sporting phenomenon since World Series Cricket was unveiled to a bemused public back in 1977. For two years World Series and Establishment cricket took place side by side in direct competition. Establishment cricket attracted the traditional audience to watch what was in effect an Australian Second XI struggle, first against India in 1977/78 and then against England the following year. To begin with the new order did not attract many spectators. While a deafening advertising campaign went on in the background, most of the world's leading players were gathered together under one roof and then unleashed in strange colours and in strange places. The Sydney Showground, which becomes the temporary home of David Bowie and Elton John and others when they visit Australia, the VFL Park, a concrete edifice for Australian Rules Football far out in the Melbourne suburb of Waverley, Football Park in Adelaide, and Gloucester Park, the home of trotting races, in Perth were all requisitioned and turned for a short while into cricket grounds. They were strange venues in the same way that Lord's Cricket Ground would leave traditional Rugby Union supporters a trifle uneasy at first if their game was suddenly played there instead of Twickenham, but they did their job for Kerry Packer's cricketers who were not then allowed to use the traditional grounds.

World Series Cricket was also accompanied by a television spectacular created by David Hill of Packer's Channel Nine which has taken television coverage of the game to new frontiers. More cameras than ever before were used and the presentation was slicker and more easily digestible for the casual viewer, the bloke at whom WSC was aimed. It is interesting that all Channel Nine's new ideas have since been taken up by most of the other stations in the world which cover cricket. But, of course, Channel Nine, like any other commercial station, will always have competition with a sport like cricket. The commercial breaks which are its life's blood mean that hamburgers and airlines and rent-a-car firms pop up between each over and take the place of measured comment. There are times when these interruptions are irritating and distracting to the viewer.

Then there was the WSC flagship, limited-over, night-time cricket played under floodlights in Sydney coupled with a mass of one-day international cricket played all over the country with players dressed in coloured clothes using a white ball in front of black sightscreens. The players were supplied with drinks by scantily clad models sitting on electric buggies – although the girls have subsequently disappeared. Yes, it was all incredibly different and small wonder that not only the Australian public looked at it all for a time with suspicion, but also that the traditional game's administrators and supporters threw their hands up in abject horror. I should know for I was one of them and wrote a book about the formation of World Series Cricket called *The Packer Affair* in which, in the words of Tony Greig, I 'gave them heaps'.

I was in the captain's room at the Sussex County Ground at Hove when Greig first told the Press about a guy called Kerry Packer. I well remember the chuckle he gave as he said, 'You don't know Kerry Packer. You don't want to underestimate him.' I sat at dinner in the Dragonara Hotel in Leeds with Kerry Packer, Tony Greig, Ian Chappell and several other WSC signings and administrators. It was during the Test match against Australia in 1977 and England's captain, Mike Brearley, was also there. He was sympathetic but had no wish to join WSC. I flew to Melbourne to see the first game which WSC played, at the VFL Park. In the New Year I flew back into Perth on the way from Pakistan to New Zealand and watched part of a Super-Test at Gloucester Park. Two months later I was in Georgetown, Guyana, when the West Indian Packer players pulled out of the West Indies side in protest because some of them had been dropped for the Test match against Bobby Simpson's official Australian side. The West Indies selectors were themselves forced to play a second XI. Earlier, I had been in Pakistan with the England side when the Board of Control for Cricket in Pakistan took against the WSC players when an attempt was made to bring four of them back from Australia to strengthen their side against England.

I saw more than most outsiders, although admittedly I began from a built-in position on the Establishment side. In those days the gap between the two sides was bitter and enormous. The WSC group had embarked upon their campaign with all the passionate fervour of a group of people starting a crusade. They were every bit as scathing about the Establishment as the traditionalists, who regarded the whole WSC thing as beneath contempt, were about them. I have no doubt too that if some of those who were selected by WSC had not been included, they would have become some of the loudest and most damning of critics.

World Series Cricket came from small beginnings. Dennis Lillee and Rod Marsh told their agent in Perth, Austin Robertson, that they should be earning more money from cricket. Robertson ran into his old friend and fellow Western Australian John Cornell and put the problem to him. Cornell not only acted in Paul Hogan's television series but was also involved with it in a managerial capacity and together they went to see Kerry Packer about the possibility of staging all-star matches round Australia in front of television cameras for the benefit of individual cricketers. At just that time Packer's researchers on Channel Nine had decided that exclusive coverage of Test cricket on television was a sure money winner. Accordingly Packer had gone to see the Australian Cricket Board to make an offer, and although he was prepared to pay considerably more money than the Australian Broadcasting Commission who currently had the rights to televise Australian cricket, although not exclusively, he was told that it was not desirable for the rights to be sold on an exclusive basis and was turned away. He felt that he had been treated less than well and said, in effect, 'Right, if I can't have exclusive coverage of Test matches in Australia, I will put on my own.' To do so, he was prepared to dip his hand into the biggest pocket of money the game had ever seen, but he was going to use it in direct opposition to the traditional game in Australia and anywhere else if the Establishment tried to block him. From the moment that Packer decided to put on his own Tests, a battle royal was guaranteed, although I dare say there are many people who if they had been able to look at what Packer was doing and to see the reasons behind his actions in the calmer perspective which is now possible, many reactions would have been different and the awful blood-lettings would have been avoided.

As it was, it became a battle to which almost no one remained wholly indifferent. The WSC players were accused of being money-grabbing mercenaries. The response of the traditional authorities was at once to raise the payments to players for Test matches and tours to levels which competed with WSC in the hope that it would prevent others from moving over to the WSC flag. In England, Cornhill Insurance stepped in and the success of their sponsorship both to the game and to themselves has, with the advantage of hindsight, weakened the Establishment's case simply because it has shown that the money was there. Before the advent of Packer the full commercial possibilities of the game had not been fully explored. A misguided Establishment fought and lost a most damaging High Court action against the so-called rebels. By now the formation of World Series Cricket had cost Packer more money than he would have anticipated but the result of Mr Justice Slade's judgement gave the WSC cause great publicity. In a sense WSC and its players had been martyred by the traditional game. I well remember Kerry Packer himself saying to various journalists, myself included, at the VFL Park in Melbourne the morning after the judgement had been made known, 'A lot of you fellows are jumping over the fence today.' Tony Greig was right; anyone who underestimated Kerry Packer did so at his peril. While cricket fans in Australia may not have flocked through the gates at these unlikely venues, the game was being talked about as never before and so too was Channel Nine, which was a main part of the objective. More and more television sets were being turned on throughout the country although Channel Nine could not reach all the outlying country districts. It must not be forgotten that for all the emotional involvement which I dare say affected Kerry Packer himself as much as anyone, for he had in effect pressed the win-at-all-costs button, this was and remained primarily a battle about exclusive television rights. Television screens were always more important than bums on seats.

The Establishment was scandalized by the fact that its leading players had shown no loyalty and had rushed off at the first sound of the enemy's bugle. But what the Establishment expected was more an unquestioning subservience to tradition rather than a direct loyalty. No one could deny that in 1977 Test match cricketers were being poorly paid in comparison to entertainers, for that is what they were, who played tennis and golf. Of course cricket is a game which only has a hold at Test match level in countries which were once part of the old British Empire, and that did not include the United States of America and the vast financial resources that that country brings to the other two games. By comparison, cricket was the poor relation, but even so Packer had already shown that much more money was available than the traditional authorities suspected.

Cricket was perennially short of cash, but it now began to look as if it was its own fault. As soon as the Packer threat came into the open, money was found to fight it. In a fast-changing world, cricket was one of the last sports still trying to run itself on the honour and glory motivation while entertainers everywhere else were cashing in as never before. The Packer invasion picked the game up by the scruff of the neck and dumped it unceremoniously in the latter part of the twentieth century. Again with hindsight, it seems astonishing that those who had been running the game had so isolated their thinking that they never even considered that an entrepreneur like Packer might come along and offer competition. If the administration of the game had moved forward at a pace more in keeping with the age in which the game lived, it would not have been so easy for Packer. Cricket was ripe for the taking and if it had not been Packer it would surely have been someone else, some other television mogul.

There is one aspect of the saga which probably, and understandably, stuck in the throats of the traditionalists more than any other: that was the clandestine and apparently deceitful way in which the operation was formulated and put into effect. When players were initially approached – and very few showed signs of hesitancy when asked to sign – they were paid an element of hush money. When the story was broken by Ian Wooldridge in the London *Daily Mail*, it came originally from a source which is still unknown except by Wooldridge, although an Australian player who had signed had, I believe, whispered to Alan Shiell, a cricket writer in Adelaide. In any event, there was a deafening shriek of outrage from the Establishment that any such thing should have been going on behind their backs. They complained that no one had been prepared to discuss it with them before signing and that now a knife had been stuck at their throats and they had been presented with a *fait accompli*. I can fully understand why the organizers of WSC were so determined to make sure that their plans remained secret. Cricket's administrators have never exactly been known for their liberal thinking and nor have they shown themselves anxious to compromise with rebellious or dissident thinkers. For this revolution to have had a chance of success, it necessarily had to have such an apparently dishonourable beginning.

Although rates of pay for Test cricketers, especially in Australia, were improving in 1977, Packer promised a far richer horizon. It has always been man's basic instinct to try and improve his lot and in the Western world at any rate we live in a society where it is man's inalienable right to sell his talents to the highest bidder if he is not otherwise irrevocably contracted. For all the agony their actions caused and the way in which their integrity was doubted, those cricketers signing for WSC were doing just that. It had not occurred to the respective boards of control to bind their players with any form of long-term contract because the possibility of a pirate operation on this scale had never occurred to them. The players were breaking no laws by signing for WSC and indeed Mr Justice Slade made it clear that the Establishment was breaking the law in trying to prevent them from joining WSC. Now that time has stripped away most emotion, and has enabled me to look at it in a perspective I was unable to find at the time, I do not believe that in an increasingly mercenary age any of them can be blamed for what they did. Nor, most of all, can Kerry Packer be blamed for wanting to use cricket to make money for his television network and for being prepared to risk huge amounts of money to try and guarantee success. For both the boss and the players it was a legitimate entrepreneurial exercise in spite of all the huffing and puffing that accompanied and pursued it. Packer was lucky in that the players who formed the hard core of WSC were ideal for his purpose. Ian Chappell, Dennis Lillee, Rod Marsh and Tony Greig were flamboyant and at times abrasive showmen to whose actions and ut-terances it was impossible to remain indifferent. They and others generated the publicity and what many at the time considered to be the notoriety which WSC needed to attract attention. In short, they were players and individuals who turned on television sets all over the country. The abrasive manner in which they advocated World Series Cricket was in itself news.

And now, where has all of this left the game of cricket? Unquestion-ably the battle between WSC and the Establishment which was waged as fiercely on the field as off, can be seen to have changed the game. It has become tougher, more brutal, more combative and is a game where the letter has taken over from the spirit of the law. In seven or eight years it has moved from being a leftover from the days when the amateur ethic reigned supreme and has become a front runner in an age of heavy competitive professionalism. The transitional period was swift and bruising. I now believe that the change was inevitable if the game was to keep in step with contemporary society. The speed and therefore the decisiveness with which this change came could perhaps have been longer drawn out and therefore more gentle. But if pressure is allowed to build up for a long time against the floodgates, the destruction when finally they burst is more sudden and dramatic. It is a moot point whether the force which breaks the gates is more to blame than those who put up such formidable resistance.

Whatever the authorities may say to the contrary, cricket is nowadays increasingly run by the players both on and off the field. An Australian Test umpire said to me at the start of the series between Australia and Pakistan in 1983/84 that as far as he was concerned it was the players' game and they could play it as they wanted. At first sight, this may seem a shameful abdication of duty, but is it not rather a bowing to the inevitable? At times these days umpires seem to be little more than metronomes who count tl : balls in an over. The overs are bowled as slowly as the players choose, the bowlers and fielders 'sledge' the opposing batsmen as they want, fielders appeal for catches they know are not out, when an appeal is given against the batsman he lingers and glares at the umpire to the point of ridicule, and the bowler does the same when he does not get the decision. It is very seldom the umpire says anything. I have seen Lillee throw an aluminium bat away in fury during a Test match against England in Perth. I saw him kick the Pakistan captain, Javed Miandad, after they ran into each other in another Test in Perth. I saw Trevor Chappell bowl that infamous underarm ball along the ground to Brian McKechnie of New Zealand at the Melbourne Cricket Ground to prevent the possibility of a six being hit. There was the time when Colin Croft knocked over New Zealand umpire, Fred Goodall, just after he had turned down an appeal by Croft who later claimed it was an accident. There have been other distasteful incidents. If the players concerned have received anything more than a caution from their Boards of Control, it has been a small fine which was probably suspended. On the field anything goes. Off the field, the players do not think twice about going to the courts crying 'restraint of trade' if they feel they have been harshly dealt with.

Undoubtedly, WSC has been held responsible for much of this. But then when WSC embraced the world's leading cricketers in 1977, it was a much more violent age than, say, 1957. It is as far-fetched to suggest that Ray Lindwall and Keith Miller would have behaved like Lillee as it is to say that Ken Rosewall would have indulged in the excesses which we have all had to endure from John McEnroe. Twenty years ago society would not have tolerated such behaviour. Nowadays, it not only tolerates it, but sometimes shows an alarming desire to want to join in. WSC did not start modern trends of behaviour on the cricket field. Tony Greig was fielding almost in the batsman's hip pocket and letting him know what he thought of him well before 1977; Dennis Lillee was hating umpires and batsmen and abusing both earlier than this; Rod Marsh was having his say too and by 1977 Ian Chappell had become quite good at dropping his trousers. It was 1972 when John Snow charged Sunny Gavaskar at Lord's.

It is true that WSC had them all together under one roof and if behaviour of this sort attracted publicity to WSC, so much the better. WSC was taking on the Establishment, it was a battle of new versus old, and the more outrageous and avant-garde the new could be, the sharper the contrast and the better it suited WSC since it resulted in more television sets being turned on. All the WSC players identified strongly with their cause and the more they upset the Establishment the happier it made them. When they all first came together in Australia they were lectured by John Newcombe and Ron Barassi, the Australian Rules Football manager who is a legend in Melbourne, on how to behave as personalities and how to put themselves over as individuals to the public. Ian Chappell had a habit of putting his hand on his box before taking up his stance. He was encouraged to do this and television came in close when he did. No wonder, when the two sides of the argument came together in a truce which at first was uneasy, at the start of the 1979/80 season in Australia, the WSC element were ever eager to indulge in on-field activities which the Establishment would not like. It was their way of making a point and who can blame them? No, modern behaviour was not invented by World Series Cricket, but it was useful to their cause.

The fusion of the two warring parties has gone on since 1979, but I still feel that the two sides are there. I think the former WSC players all felt that they were rather more equal than the Establishment players who had not been selected by WSC. Now, with the retirement of Lillee, Marsh and Greg Chappell, Kepler Wessels remains as the last WSC player in the Australia side, and lines will, I am sure, no longer be drawn up for WSC or non-WSC reasons. However, I do not think that behaviour will change, even though Marsh and Lillee, who have retired, were two such important protagonists of the new order. Society in Australia will not change just because these two are no longer playing cricket for their country. The outward and visible evidence of the split caused by WSC will still be apparent in media circles.

Although the Australian Broadcasting Commission are now allowed limited competition with Channel Nine, primarily because Channel Nine does not reach into all the corners of Australia. Channel Nine is very much the first among equals and as such is a reminder of the split.

But 1983/84 in Australia will be remembered not for its eminently forgettable cricket, but because it was the last season in which Greg Chappell, Dennis Lillee and Rod Marsh played for Australia. Three of the greatest cricketers of this or any other generation, they have all had a profound effect on the cricketing fortunes of their country. All three of them were born with a genius which they developed to the fullest extent. They each took their own game to a point where it became an art form and as cricketers they will all three always be talked about in the same breath. It happens that they were also among the staunchest supporters of Kerry Packer and indeed Marsh and Lillee had, as I have shown, something to do with the start of WSC. Their disappearance from the scene of contemporary cricket hails the end of an extraordinary era in Australia which has seen the game reach and maintain hitherto unknown levels of popularity and therefore prosperity. Their departure will leave cricket the poorer on the field and their influence from a technical viewpoint at any rate will always remain. The end of the Chappell, Lillee and Marsh era is as good a time as any to try and take stock and see exactly what has come out of Kerry Packer's brainchild, World Series Cricket. I have watched each of the last six seasons in Australia since the truce and have seen how the game has developed. I wrote *The Packer Affair* from an entrenched position from which I thought that little good could come from WSC and that it had changed cricket irrevocably and for the worse. Six years later I would like say that, for better or worse, the game's evolution was probably inevitable.

2
Consequences

The balance-sheet of World Series Cricket must be looked at primarily in terms of Australia for it was an exercise designed by an Australian television mogul determined to use Test Cricket in Australia to his company's advantage. The objective was to make money inside Australia and if Kerry Packer had not been a shrewd business man of extraordinary tenacity, with a stubborn determination not to be beaten and with the financial backing of the Channel Nine network, the idea might easily have been stillborn. It was, sure and simple, an Australian commercial venture by a man who, quite early in the story, formed a strong and indivisible loyalty to those who joined in his crusade. He was determined, at whatever cost, to win his fight to gain the exclusive rights to televise Test cricket in Australia and he was just as anxious to repay the players' loyalty to him. This last sentiment was most strongly understood by all who signed for WSC and will have been an important reason why so many cricketers signed willingly in the first instance, prepared to put their cricketing lives on the table. For Kerry Packer, this extra involvement gave the whole project a personal and emotional base. But it still remained essentially an Australian operation even if he looked overseas for operatives who would help make it work. It all made sound commercial sense. Out of this was born Packer's much publicized 'Devil take the hindmost' philosophy.

Then, of course, he was dealing with and taking on something which was both an institution and a tradition. I dare say that there was no battle Packer would have enjoyed more than a head-on collision with the Establishment. Emotional waves of bitter hostility came flooding back from all round the cricket-playing world. When there is emotion on both sides, overreaction and hasty misjudgement almost invariably follow. The game of cricket was the poor old Aunt Sally caught up in between. Now, seven years on, it is possible to sit back and take a more rational view of the game of cricket as it now is, and a more objective look at all the disruptions it suffered.

First of all, and I think this was true all over the cricket-playing world, the advent of WSC gave the game a greater celebrity, a wider public awareness, than it had ever had before, especially in Australia where thousands and thousands of people, being unable to avoid the publicity the issue was given, were shaken into talking and thinking about it. They met the story daily in the news bulletins on radio and television and endlessly on the front pages of their newspapers. Channel Nine itself was also receiving tremendous publicity, which was fair enough for this was the original objective, although by now it was proving to be an expensive pursuit.

It is true that the lot of the Test cricketer was better in Australia than in any other country before the formation of WSC and it was still improving. The excellent sponsorship of Benson & Hedges had been one of the main reasons for this. Also the popularity of the game was increasing after successive visits by England in 1974/75 and the West Indies in 1975/76 when Lillee and Thomson bowled Australia to massive victories in both series. The 'gates' had been big and these two seasons were followed by a short series against Pakistan in 1976/77 which, thanks to Imran Khan's bowling in Sydney, was also a success. Then, in March 1977, came the greatest showpiece the game has ever known, the Centenary Test match in which Australia beat England by 45 runs which, by an extraordinary coincidence was Australia's exact margin of victory in the first-ever Test match a hundred years earlier. The game appeared never to have been stronger and yet while that match was in progress the shadow of Kerry Packer lurked in the corridors of the pavilion at the MCG, although we did not know it at the time. By then, Packer was after the right to televise cricket on Channel Nine on an exclusive basis and had been turned down by the Australian Cricket Board. The fact that the game was prospering made those rights even more alluring. Packer decided to put on his own Tests and while the traditionalists recoiled in horror, the uncommitted will have said of Packer in true Australian fashion, when they were allowed to see what he was trying to do, 'Good on yer mate, give it a go.' He gave it a go on a grand scale and although this new audience may not have ventured through the turnstiles until they had seen what it was like, you can bet anything that curiosity got the better of them and they switched on their television sets. The moment each set was turned on, WSC had scored a victory.

The Australian Cricket Board, who had the support of the International Cricket Conference in the shape of a letter from Charles Palmer, that year's president, authorising them to find a solution if they could – a fact not widely known at the time and certainly not by myself when I wrote *The Packer Affair* – were the prime movers in looking for a truce. Five years later, in 1983/84, Pakistan played a most disappointing Test series and then the West Indies made up the numbers for the Benson & Hedges World Series Cup and the gate receipts from eighteen one-day games approached three million Australian dollars and goodness knows how many television viewers watched as well. The impetus the game was given by WSC is still there and is probably increasing. The proprietor of Channel Nine and the treasurer of the Australian Cricket Board must both be happy men.

Before WSC came on the scene, one-day cricket had made little impact in Australia and had not been seized upon as the financial saviour of cricket as it had in England where there were already three domestic one-day competitions. WSC pinned its faith on one-day international cricket and its impact was sensational. It may from the outset have drawn a noticeably different crowd from that which came to watch Test cricket, but none the less it caught hold of the public imagination to an astonishing extent. It seemed to fulfil a social need. The stage has long since gone where its pull can be accounted for in terms of novelty value. A one-day international match brings together twenty-two of the world's best cricketers and is a product which has a finite end after a hundred overs of constant excitement. The new audience which this type of cricket has attracted does not give a damn that it may cause a serious drop in the overall standards of the game. It is no concern of theirs and why should it be? They are being offered a product which has to stand comparison with television, the cinema, the beach, pop music, disco dancing and beer drinking and any other form of popular entertainment. It has been packaged enticingly and cleverly marketed. The public like it and want more of it. It is a simple equation. One-day cricket may be pop cricket, but it was designed simply and solely to increase the popularity of the game and as such has been an unqualified success. It was not until the 1984/85 season which ended with the World Championship of Cricket that there were any signs that the public were being given too much of this type.

One-day cricket was not the invention of those who thought up

World Series Cricket; they merely took the idea and adapted it to suit Australia. The major invention for which WSC can claim credit is the introduction of night cricket played under floodlights. It began during the first year of WSC when they played at the Sydney Showground, which was regarded by some of the *habitués* over the wall at the Sydney Cricket Ground as a leper colony. The following year, 1978/79, the Trustees of the SCG allowed World Series Cricket to use the ground and Kerry Packer inspired the building of the six huge floodlight pylons round the ground. Of course, they are unsightly, but by now they have become accepted by most people and night matches are extraordinarily popular. Naturally, there are some traditionalists who still dislike them although even they will surely have to admit that cricket played under floodlights is a wonderful spectacle. Lights which are even more effective were put up at the Melbourne Cricket Ground for the World Championship of Cricket in March 1985 which was played as part of the celebrations signalling the 150th anniversary of the founding of the state of Victoria. Attempts have been made to play cricket under floodlights on football grounds in England although I doubt if night cricket will ever be an unqualified success in England because of the uncertain climate. Night cricket has also been played at the athletic stadium just outside Bridgetown in Barbados and most cricket-playing countries are exploring the possibilities.

Since the peace treaty in 1979, official cricket in Australia has been marketed by a company owned by Packer, PBL Marketing presided over by Lynton Taylor. They have made a success of the job too, as they have promoted the game and have taken advantage of all the commercial opportunities international cricket offers in Australia. Their methods will not have suited everyone, just as the marketing policy of the Test & County Cricket Board in England has not suited everyone, and there are those who think they could have done it better. But this is the world of commerce where the competition is nothing if not tough. In a sense, PBL Marketing has been the frontrunner, showing the way and raising a good deal of money in the process. The fact has got to be faced that we live in the mid-1980s. Surely we should not be squeamish about that?

As a result of all this, Australia's Test match and international cricketers are being paid good money. When he retired, Greg Chappell said that they were not being paid nearly enough, but that is the normal reaction of most people whatever their jobs. Elsewhere in the world Test match fees have risen enormously since WSC came into existence and the money has come mostly from increased sponsorship. World Series Cricket has shown the traditional authorities the commercial possibilities of the game. Paradoxically, although the West Indians were central to the success of WSC, it has indirectly imposed an almost intolerable burden on the West Indies Test players. The West Indies Cricket Board of Control has for a long time been desperately short of money to the point of bankruptcy. The reason is simply that it is the only country which is unable to make money out of its home series. The Caribbean is a vastly expensive up-market holiday area, there are huge distances to be travelled and only two of their Test grounds hold more than 12,000 spectators. Also there is a limit to what populations with a low *per capita* income can be charged to watch Test cricket. The West Indies therefore rely heavily on the money they make from tours in England and Australia to keep them solvent. Foreign Exchange cannot be taken out of India and Pakistan. In Australia, the West Indies are especially popular and generate more money than any other side and probably deserve more than they get paid in return. World Series Cricket brought much more money into the pockets of the West Indians, and now to try and ensure that the players continue to receive a big annual income and are not tempted by offers from South Africa, their Board of Control has arranged the most punishing programme ever devised which stretches through until 1990. It is as well that those tiny islands seem to have an unlimited reservoir of natural talent for the likelihood must be that some of their leading players will burn themselves out before their time.

To keep payments high is one of the reasons so much Test cricket is played today. With only seven countries involved, the fear must be that one day saturation point will be reached. I would have expected this to have happened first of all in Australia with its heavy programme each summer, and in 1984/85 a sequence of thirty-one consecutive one-day internationals produced signs that there is a limit to how much even the Australian public can take, although the television audience may have been unaffected. Spectators at games are no longer all-important, it is the customers at home who turn on their television sets and therefore watch the commercials who count the most. And maybe from the depths of an armchair saturation point never comes. If it should come, cricket would be in mortal danger for the moguls like Kerry Packer might suddenly lose interest and back away, and it is frightening to think where that would leave the game. In my view, though, Kerry Packer and Channel Nine's recipe for success and prosperity will bear fruit for some time to come and provide a financial bulwark to minimize the dangers if the public taste should change.

I have got the impression in Australia that one-day cricket is promoted and thrives at the expense of Test cricket, but this may be an impression given by the reaction of the public to one-day cricket. In any event such an approach could be justified by the figures on the balance-sheet. It is hard to answer back to the figure of nearly three million Australian dollars as gate receipts for the 1983/84 World Series Cup. Undoubtedly, the contemporary liking for one-day cricket has caused standards of play to fall which is sad, but this was happening in other parts of the world, most of all in England, a long time before WSC had been heard of. In any event, it is no use having high standards if they do not produce enough money to pay the bills. Every age gets the cricket it deserves and this is the pop age which demands a different product. Kerry Packer and his advisers were clever enough to spot what Australians wanted and to give it to them.

Standards of behaviour on the field and off have fallen considerably, but as I have tried to show in the last chapter that had nothing to do with WSC. It is a sad fact of life that the kind of incidents to which I have referred make good television. I wonder how many times Lillee's kick at Javed Miandad was seen on television. All these incidents after they have been blown up by television give the game greater publicity in an age when all publicity is good publicity.

With the rewards for winning so much larger these days, umpires are put under greater pressure than ever before, but Kerry Packer and WSC did not invent that in 1977. Crowd violence is another modern phenomenon which has been highlighted by events on the Hill and outside the ground after the close of play in the night games in Sydney. But no one can say that this, or the extrovert behaviour in Bay Thirteen in Melbourne, has been WSC inspired. Look what was happening at some of the John Player League games in England on Sunday afternoons, and it is longer ago than that that West Indian crowds, inspired by acute disappointment and the rum bottle in equal measure, have gone over the top and held up Test matches. Yes, international cricket does have to be more carefully and more thoroughly policed these days, but Australia is not the only country where that happens and the signs were there long before WSC.

When it all began in 1977, I was in the vanguard of those who thought that Kerry Packer and his cohorts were ogres all set to destroy the game. Now it is my opinion that Packer and his advisers were foresighted enough to see that the rapid advance of society had left cricket behind. He saw the opportunities it offered him and could only have been surprised at the readiness with which he was taken up by the world's leading players. The signs were all there, he had read them accurately, and he brought the game into step with the society which nourished it. At the moment, I believe that we are seeing cricket shake itself out as it comes to terms with a process of change which would anyway have been forced upon it. I have tried to show that so much of what was happening, the blame for which was laid at Packer's door, was already beginning to happen as part of an evolutionary process. My case is that if Kerry Packer had never been invented, the game of cricket which would have been played in 1987 would have been almost exactly the same as that which will now be played in 1987. Kerry Packer has been successful and has made lots of money simply by giving a natural evolutionary process, which had temporarily stuttered, a shrewd push in the back. And who is to blame him for that? Tony Greig had warned us that it would be dangerous to underestimate him.

3
The Lure of the West Indies

Since the peace treaty in 1979, the Australian Cricket Board has played its financial cards pretty close to its chest. Very few people know how much money Packer and Channel Nine paid the board for the exclusive right to televise official cricket in Australia and I am not one of them, but it is fair to assume that it was a hefty sum. Since that date the gate receipts, the Benson & Hedges sponsorship and other income should have guaranteed a healthy balance on the right side of the line. The most powerful single outside influence to generate money for the ACB has surely been the West Indians. They have been coming to Australia more frequently than any other of the Test-playing countries. Their visit in 1984/85 was the fourth in six seasons.

No other cricketers seem to catch the imagination in the same way as the West Indians. Their image as the world's most exciting cricketers was built up when they were introduced to Test cricket more than fifty years ago by the unpredictable genius of one extraordinary man, Learie Constantine. No batsman had hit the ball so flamboyantly and so thrillingly before Constantine, no one had bowled with energy which was so frenetic as to seem to add yards to his pace, and perhaps no one had played cricket at this level who was so engagingly cheerful. But even allowing for all this, it was his fielding which counted for the greater part of the essence of Constantine which was unconsciously distilled first into a legend around one man and was then transferred to become the collective image for all West Indian cricketers.

In fact, the legend of Constantine was based on surprisingly few mind-boggling performances. Yet people held their breath at the very mention of his name. My own mother, no born devotee of cricket although she bravely learned to tolerate it on my behalf, insisted that one of the labrador puppies which came to Hoveton should be called Learie for it was so fiendishly agile in pursuit of a ball or indeed anything else. Constantine, too, was performing his deeds when black men were much rarer in England than they are today and this added to the fascination and maybe the charismatic charm of the man. He was always friendliness itself when I was privileged to know him as a member of the press-box towards the end of his life.

West Indian cricketers are therefore traditionally expected to bowl faster and to hit the ball harder than anyone else. They are expected to blast their way out of danger always with broad grins on their faces which should reflect the fun-loving tropical islands they are supposed to have come from. They must field with a joyous panache and walk with that unmistakeable lilt which is so impossible to copy. They must talk in that rhythmical melodious voice which suggests they spend their lives singing calypsoes and dancing the Jump-Up, the carnival dance. Instinctively, they do all of these things and when they play cricket these attributes make them alluring and compelling to watch. In the fifties and sixties at any rate, and probably still today, there is a strong element about them of Harry Belafonte in white flannel trousers.

But as so often happens when images are preconceived, the actuality falls some way short of the dream. Test cricket is a hard game and the West Indians are not on top of the pile by chance. The present generation of West Indian Test cricketers may have worked even harder than their predecessors to develop and perfect their talents, although I doubt if anyone worked much harder at the same process than Clyde Walcott, Frank Worrell and Everton Weekes, to name three. Cricket today is all about winning and to win consistently calls for ruthlessness and dedication. These are qualities that the present West Indians as a unit have developed to greater levels than ever before. Historically, the West Indians have always been capable of stirring deeds, but consistency was not one of their qualities. Too often, impetuosity and the devil-may-care attitude which caused the West Indies cricketing legend to be formed, led them to squander their own rich talents and to end up as the nice guys who came second.

This wanton wastefulness started to end under the guidance of Frank Worrell, who captained the side in the early sixties. Gary Sobers then did his best until the passing years caught up with the sensational talents of the side he inherited from Worrell. Now, Clive Lloyd, that genial puppet-master who is never outwardly ruffled, has welded a new generation of West Indians into the most efficient cricketing unit the Caribbean has ever produced. He may have banished for ever the days when opponents of the West Indies could sit back and wait for these highly able and individual cricketers to beat themselves.

There is still a joyous infection about much of their cricket as there could hardly fail to be from players who come from such an uninhibited and spontaneous part of the world. But the West Indians have at last learned that a seven-hour century can be crucially important in the context of some Test matches; so too can be the constant battering-ram of four fast bowlers getting through twelve or thirteen overs an hour; they know about sledging and putting umpires under pressure and all the other tricks of the trade. They would be crazy not to for that is the way the game is played in this commercial age. But still the individual performances of Viv Richards whether batting or fielding – has cricket ever produced better entertainment than an innings by Richards at his best? – Malcolm Marshall bowling and batting, Clive Lloyd and Gordon Greenidge batting, Joel Garner and Michael Holding bowling, are in step with the tradition which Learie Constantine created so many years ago. For the most part, they keep it fresh and immediate and ensure that the West Indies deserve the crowds which come to see them play. Whether they or their Board of Control have been amply rewarded for what they have done for the game round the world over the last two decades, is another and more difficult question.

The West Indies image has to begin at home just as it began in the streets of Port of Spain for Learie Constantine so long ago. In those days at the turn of the century he and his friends devoted every moment of their time to playing cricket in the streets or on any open piece of ground they could find with makeshift bats and balls, but with an unquenchable excitement and enthusiasm for the game which has not abated one iota in the Caribbean in the intervening eighty years. My favourite memory of the West Indies comes from a roughly similar scene. I was in Georgetown, Guyana, for the Fifth Test match between England and the West Indies in late March and early April 1968. Guyana is part of the South American mainland and while Georgetown itself and the sugar estates are pure West Indies, with a lot of colonial Dutch architecture thrown in, the interior is Amazon country and South America.

During the rest day of the Test match I wandered out of the Park Hotel which later acquired fame as the last civilized habitat of Abdul

Malik, otherwise known as Michael X, before he was arrested and hung for murder. I turned left down Main Street, over the level crossing and down to the sea wall where the Pegasus Hotel now stands. I walked along the wall for about a mile and not only was the beach the colour of mud, but the sea itself was brown. This is caused by the vast quantities of silt which are washed down the three huge rivers which flow out into the sea from Guyana – the Demerara, the Essequibo and the Berbice rivers. It was a most unappetizing sea shore. While I was walking a car pulled up ahead of me and discharged five or six small boys who leapt over the wall onto the mud-coloured sand carrying what passed for a cricket bat and some stumps. I watched while they measured out the pitch and began to play. One boy seized the bat, another got ready to bowl and there was a wicket-keeper while the others fielded on either side of the pitch. The batsman took guard, the bowler ran in, the batsman played a stroke and the leg-side fielder gave chase and dropped his hand on the ball and the batsman stopped running. This must have gone on for some time since they were still playing when later I retraced my steps. The game was accompanied by screams and yells of excitement, and in all ways but one it was an entirely normal scene especially in the West Indies. The only difference between what I was watching and thousands of similar scenes in the cricket-playing world was that it was all mime. They had no ball.

At first it seemed so sad, for Guyana is a poor country and any sort of ball would almost certainly have been much too expensive. But then I realized that the boys were enormously happy and were enjoying themselves so much that it did not matter that they had no ball. If you knew you could not really be out maybe it was more fun pretending to be Sobers or Kanhai although perhaps not quite such fun to be a bowler and to remain wicketless. I wondered if the game of cricket could ever have had a better exercise in public relations. This story illustrates perfectly the hold the game has on the people in that part of the world.

When I first went to the Caribbean I found it strange, and I think I still do, that excitable, volatile people who live for much of the time in emotional extremes should have taken so all-embracingly to cricket and have made it the national game in countries which were once the old British West Indies. Obviously it all began when the locals picked the game up from the British garrisons and settlers, but I would have thought that they would have been better suited by something faster with more physical contact involved. Logically, perhaps football should have provided the answer. Yet when you freeze cricket at any given moment, it is essentially a game with a permanent one against one situation. It is the bowler and batsman or batsman and fielder who are in direct combat. I had only to watch the first few overs of the first Test match I ever saw in the Caribbean to realize that this was perhaps the main reason why cricket has such a hold in this part of the world. This particular Test match was the first in the series between the West Indies and England in 1967/68 and was played at Queen's Park Oval, Port of Spain, which is one of the two or three most beautiful Test grounds in the world. England batted first and Wes Hall and Charlie Griffith steamed in to bowl to John Edrich and Geoff Boycott who were soon ducking and weaving for their very lives. The big crowd cheered and laughed themselves hoarse as they revelled in every delivery. I shall never forget the spectators standing behind the wire fencing just to the right of the press-box singing Calypso Rose's 1968 carnival hit, 'Fire in your Wire' as Hall raced to the wicket. The whole scene was quintessentially West Indian.

In their different ways all the islands and territories which form the cricketing West Indies have their own distinctive characteristics. Guyana is the poorest and life there is not especially glamorous, yet in Georgetown I have met some of the kindest people I have come across anywhere in the world. It is a country of fascinating contrasts and there is so much to see including the Kaiteur Falls which is said to be the tallest waterfall in the world, and the cathedral in Georgetown which is the highest wooden building in the world. The government of Forbes Burnham is negro orientated and leans substantially towards the beliefs of Karl Marx while the heavy Indian population which mans the sugar estates comes off a poor third. Yet the innate West Indian sense of fun is never far below the surface as I found in many evenings spent dancing and drinking at the Belvedere or watching spectators climb into the 'free' seats in the trees outside the ground behind the commentary boxes at Bourda, the Test ground. I saw perhaps the most irresistible of all the calypso concerts I have been to at the Old Globe Theatre in Georgetown when the Mighty Sparrow was the star of the evening and his calypso hit for that year was 'Good Morning Mr Walker'; it was all about a guy who married a girl for her bank book and not her looks. It was a scream and had a very catchy tune.

Trinidad with its oil is a rich industrial island with an exciting cosmopolitan population which reflects the frequency with which it has changed hands since the days of the Spanish Main. Each subsequent conqueror left his mark which you can still see in the faces of some of the population. Trinidad is the home of traditional West Indian culture and the fusion of races has left the islanders with a strong imaginative streak which is reflected most particularly at each year's carnival on the two days before the start of Lent. Port of Spain's carnival may be thought by some to come second by a short head to that in Rio which I have not had the luck to see, but perhaps those who think that have never visited Port of Spain at carnival time. For two days the entire population goes on the most enormous bender. The city is awash with music as the bands parade up and down the streets playing that year's selection of tunes. A Trinidad band at carnival time may number as many as 400 people for all the supporters count as the band. Each band has a theme for the year and the supporters all dress themselves accordingly whether the theme is from history or from space fiction or something in between. The carnival dance is the jump-up and for non-West Indians it is frustrating. When the locals do it, it is beautifully rhythmical and effortless, but let a European try and imitate them and it looks terrible. There is something of the jump-up about West Indian cricketers in the field. For the two days of carnival everyone is equal and it is all unadulterated joy. But 'progress' has not left Trinidad entirely untouched. When I was there in 1980 I went one evening to the Mighty Shadow's calypso tent and as I was walking back along Frederick Street towards the Savannah I was mugged. The police later told me they were sure my assailants were Venezuelans who come across to mug at carnival time. I am quite sure they were not Trinidadians – at least I hope they were not. Trinidad is the island of the three Cs: cricket, carnival and calypso. Well, maybe four, for the crumpet is as breathtaking as any I have seen anywhere in the world.

Barbados is everyone's idea of the perfect tropical island. Tourism is its main industry and the beaches along the west coast are among the finest in the world. Real estate on the west coast fetches gold mine prices. Barbados remained English from the time the English first arrived in 1625 until the island gained independence in the 1960s. As a result there is little mixed blood there and it is peopled by two races, the English and the descendants of the Africans who arrived in the horrific days of the slave trade. Nowadays, although the outskirts of Bridgetown have attracted a number of factories and other outward signs of industry, it is a lovely gentle seafaring town. The Careenage in the middle is pure Treasure Island. A small arrowhead of water leads off the main bay and provides Bridgetown with its old domestic harbour. The schooners with their masts and rigging etched against the sky and tied up at the quay on each side of the water create much of the atmosphere, and there are always groups of local fishermen as well as tourists hanging over the parapet of the old bridge which crosses the Careenage. Sailors standing on the decks throw coins which glint momentarily in the sunlight before they hit the water and immediately children dive after the bounty and one comes up grinning from ear to ear with a small coin between thumb and forefinger. The little square on the same side of the bridge as the parliament house is called Trafalgar Square with its own small statue of Nelson who spent a fair amount of time in the Caribbean.

About a mile over the bridge on the other side of the Careenage, on the left just before the racecourse, Harry's Nitery deals with the carnal curiosity of the tourists. On the upstairs floor the cabaret introduces the Caribbean in all its nakedness. Harry himself is sadly dead and I daresay the atmosphere of the old days when Harry used to introduce his own cabaret will never return. Harry, who was of African origin, spoke English as if he had been educated at Eton or Oxford and probably both. He assured his audience which was packed in like sardines as his henchmen extracted every last dollar piece – they were even standing on the balcony which overlooked the street – that they were about to witness scenes of extraordinary and almost biblical beauty. As I remember it, he brought in Adam and Eve on a number of occasions. When the great moment arrived it all seemed to me to be fairly basic, but Harry was undoubtedly a considerable earner of foreign exchange. On one occasion he was had up either for living on immoral earnings or for keeping a house of low repute. However, the judge realized his importance to the community, and Harry was sentenced to one day's imprisonment which was to end when the court rose which it did immediately.

I have spent a number of days driving round the island, usually in the capable hands of Gibbons, a taxi driver who does duty as the chauffeur of the famous English cricket writer Jim Swanton when he is in the island. Gibbons has a card which describes him as a 'courteous and efficient' taxi driver. His courtesy is too perfect for words and I only wish that the efficiency of his clutch was in the same class. Gibbons almost invariably wears a dark green homburg hat and he has the charming habit of raising it, which he does on every possible occasion, with great deliberation, but from the back.

A drive round the island shows Barbados to be a charmingly sleepy agricultural island away from the bustle of Bridgetown and the artificial pulse rate of the west coast. Interminable seas of sugar cane wave inevitably in the wind as the narrow road takes you to Crane beach, on to Sam Lord's Castle, once the home of the buccaneer who deliberately shipwrecked every vessel that came in sight of that corner of the island where the seas are so treacherous. His regency Gothic house is now a luxurious hotel. Then it is on to Codrington College with its handsome avenue of King palms in the district of Bathsheba known as Little Scotland and finally to Farley Hill where the old plantation house, now burnt down, was used for the film *Island in the Sun*. Everywhere we went, in every village or in the country if there were two or three boys together, they were playing cricket and were busy being Sobers or Hall or Griffith. Often their pitch was the middle of the road too. There was one glorious scene when the village barber was cutting a boy's hair as he sat on a chair in the open air and he kept jumping up to go and join in the game of cricket which was going on nearby. Each time a firm hand pulled him back.

Jamaica is the largest of the islands and also the most beautiful, but it is a country of startling and alarming contrasts. The fashionable north coast, which was so popular with Americans before Manley came to power in Jamaica and which picked up again when Seaga ousted the Manley Government, has all the tourist gloss and those of the world's best beaches which are not to be found in Barbados. The north coast, glamorous and hugely expensive, runs almost from Negril, past Round Hill to Montego Bay, to Discovery Bay to Ocho Rios where the Jamaica Inn reigns supreme and onto the banana port of Oracabessa, the spiritual home of Belafonte's Day-O, where Ian Fleming, the creator of James Bond, had a house called Goldeneye. The road winds on to Port Maria with Nöel Coward's first house, Blue Harbour, on the left between the road and the sea, and his second where he died and is buried in the garden, Firefly Hill, up the hill on the other side of the road with its spectacular view of the bay and the mountains leading to Kingston. It was the actress Lynne Fontaine who said that she could hardly bring herself to look at the mountains from Coward's garden for they reminded her of rows and rows and rows of empty theatre seats. The road ends at Port Antonio.

Kingston, a jumble of a city, lies in the south of the island. The northern suburbs are smart and well-to-do but the city grows more dirty and crowded and has a horrifying crime rate. Beyond Kingston to the west lies Spanish Town, which has the same problems and if anything in even more exaggerated form. At the end of the long cause-way stretching out to sea on the other side of Kingston is Port Royal, once the infamous city of Morgan, one of the most successful of all pirates. Port Royal was destroyed by an earthquake and what remains is little more than a ghostly skeleton. Kingston also boasts Sabina Park which used to be the smallest Test match ground in the world, but is now being rebuilt and enlarged. This was where Wes Hall almost pushed himself off the sightscreen as he started his run and where, in 1957/58, Gary Sobers made the highest ever individual Test score of 365 not out against Pakistan. It was also here in February 1968 that the West Indies looked like being beaten by England in the Second Test, the crowd rioted and the police had to use tear gas to bring the situation under control.

The Recreation Ground in St John's Antigua has only been a Test match ground for four years, yet it is appropriate that the main ground on an island which has produced Viv Richards, Andy Roberts and now Richie Richardson should have been given Test match status. Strangely, it was a Russian Jew, a Mr Rapaport who lives in Switz-erland, who provided the money to build more stands. The sugar industry in Antigua is no longer profitable and very run down, which leaves tourism as the major dollar-earner. St John's is another slow-moving town although when I was last there in 1980 it came to life in the most remarkable way to celebrate the wedding of Viv Richards who himself celebrated the occasion by taking a hundred off England in the first Test match played in the island.

A visit to the Nelson's Harbour in Antigua, a glorious natural har-bour which provided a semi-permanent home for Nelson's fleet when it was in the Caribbean, and still almost perfectly preserved, takes tourists back to the late eighteenth century. My own favourite spot in Antigua is the Lord Nelson Club, a small hotel on the sea front near the airport. It has very few rooms and it is far off the main tourist track with the same people going back year after year. It has the most delightful small bar and in so many ways it is pure Hemingway.

The neighbouring island of Montserrat, which is volcanic with black beaches and so not overrun with tourists, is the unlikely home of George Martin's recording studios. Paul McCartney had been in resid-ence shortly before I arrived there and Stevie Wonder was currently

recording. The islands which form the Leewards are all quite delightful. Further south, the Windwards have not yet produced cricketers to
compare with Richards and company, but St Vincent, St Lucia, Dom-
inica and the ill-fated Grenada are all tropical paradises. Grenada is
the most beautiful, St Lucia is my favourite, but there is really little to
choose between any of them. In all of them tourism and the Yankee
dollar play an important part and so too does cricket. It was Frank
Worrell who said that he thought the great West Indian cricketers of
the future would come from the smaller islands, and so far the Leewards have proved him at any rate partially right. I remember that the
ground staff at the delightful ground set in a mango grove in Castries
in St Lucia were all women, and when it rained they came on with
brushes to sweep the water away. One morning I drank rum and
coconut water with the first Lord Mayor Castries had had for over a
hundred years; delicious it was too. Then there was Nelson our taxi
driver. Whenever I told him anything he would turn round with a
lovely grin and say, 'That I do believe.' I have been lucky enough to
visit the Caribbean eight times and never for a single moment have I
been bored.

4
A New Season

Every cricket tour is a self-contained adventure. I have been on more than thirty overseas tours and each one has left its own special memories. I have always felt that what actually happens on the field of play is only fifty per cent of any tour. On the other side of the boundary there are the many people I have met and the friends I have made, there are the exciting parts of the world I have visited and all the adventures I have had. Away from the cricket, the most exciting time was the month I spent in five Latin American countries as assistant manager of a tour arranged by Derrick Robins in March 1979, and the most extraordinary was a few days' cricket played in the main square in Corfu Town. On 6 October 1976 five of us left a lock-up garage almost underneath the Albert Hall in London in a 1921 Rolls Royce and a new 3.5 litre Rover and during the next forty-six days and nights we drove to Bombay, arriving just in time for Johnny Woodcock and myself to start reporting the 1976/77 tour of India by MCC. Then, there have been all the happenings in the Test-playing countries which have stretched from visiting the Taj Mahal in Agra, going down a gold mine in Kalgoorlie, a diamond mine in Kimberley, watching the world champion sheep-shearer in action one evening in Alexandra in the South Island of New Zealand and the world champion axeman at the Royal Sydney Agricultural show, and taking part in a wild boar hunt fifty miles west of Lahore, which I have described in detail later in the book. And there have been more excitements along the way than I can possibly remember.

'Back for another season then, are you mate?' smiled the immigration chap at Sydney Airport on 16 October 1983 as he handed me back my passport. I struggled into a taxi with my bags – in Sydney most taxi drivers still seem to be Australian while in Melbourne they are invariably Greek – and we had only just got clear of the airport when I was subjected to a fearsome interrogation about Geoff Boycott. The Sunday newspapers I found in the shop at the Sheraton-Wentworth Hotel were hotly debating the Australian captaincy. Bob Hawke looked as if he was heading for trouble with his own Labour party over uranium mining, and the forecasters were promising a wet summer. It all sounded too familiar for words, and nice and homely at the same time.

I never thought it would be much of a season's cricket unless a miracle occurred and the stress fracture to Imran Khan's left shin suddenly mended. Without his bowling Pakistan did not have a worthwhile chance of beating Australia. He had not bowled for Pakistan in the World Cup in England in 1983 and had only bowled on two occasions for Sussex after that. But since the English season had ended he had played in an exhibition match in Kingston Jamaica and had scored a hundred, so perhaps there was just a chance. He had made himself unavailable for the short tour of India which preceded the trip to Australia, and the drawn series under Zaheer Abbas's captaincy had received mixed reports. Anyway, the Pakistan selectors, unconvinced by the prospects of Imran's fitness, had picked Zaheer to take the side to Australia. However, after the side had been announced the President of the Board of Control for Cricket in Pakistan, Air Marshal Nur Khan, appointed Imran as captain for the tour in Zaheer's place. Since Zaheer's original appointment had been reasonable enough in the absence of medical evidence that Imran would be able to play, the appointment of Imran by the Air Marshal had a political look about it for he made the decision without any medical backing. There is a strong rivalry between Karachi and Lahore. Zaheer is from Karachi and Imran's home is Lahore. Now that he was back in charge, Imran took a long look at the side he had been given and decided it would have to be changed. One of those who had originally been picked was Shoaib Muhammad, the son of Hanif, the 'little master'. Shoaib is an opening batsman like his father and had gone to India, playing in two Test matches with limited success. Through no fault of his own Shoaib had become something of a political hot potato. The chairman of the selection committee which had chosen Shoaib for India and then Australia was Asib Hasan. He had lived in Hanif's house in Karachi for a number of years, so Shoaib's selection produced obvious accusations of favouritism. Imran now decided that Shoaib should be left behind.

At the time Nur Khan brought back Imran as captain it looked as if he had made the best decision for Pakistan even if Imran was not able to bowl for the first two Test Matches. He had done a fine job since taking over the captaincy from Javed Miandad in 1982 and Zaheer had, by all accounts, been less than inspirational in India. As it appears that Imran was brought back without any medical backing, he probably let his own feelings get in the way of logic and told Nur Khan that he would be fit. He was desperately keen to take part in Pakistan's first ever five-Test tour of Australia and felt that if he was fit Pakistan would have a good chance of winning. Who is to say that he was wrong. It was asking too much therefore to have expected him to declare himself unavailable for Australia and the decision should have been made by a doctor. Although I am one of Imran's greatest supporters, I am sure that, with the advantage of hindsight, it would have been better for Pakistan if he had never gone to Australia. The dangers and confusions which stem from having what was in effect a non-playing captain are enormous, especially when the side to be captained is the national team of Pakistan, where cricket and local politics are so inextricably entwined. Zaheer may not be the best of captains, but if it had been his side all the way through there would have been a welcome continuity and the players would have known exactly where they stood.

By the time we all foregathered in Brisbane, I had spent a week in Sydney putting the finishing touches to a book with the highly improbable title of *Wine, Women and Wickets*. James Fraser, who has a publishing company in Sydney, had bravely commissioned me to write it before I left Australia the previous February – a decision he will probably live to regret. I put most of it together while sitting in a rickety wooden chair in the hot sun on the Pallas Beach in Lindos on the island of Rhodes, that is to say only 300 yards away from where I wrote this one. The three Ws is a succession of stories about some of the more unlikely occurrences in my life. I was happy with it even if when reading it James felt that he needed to wear a pair of glasses with lenses which were a trifle darker than normal!

I came to Brisbane pleased that it was over and ready for the cricket to begin. I stayed as usual at the Kangaroo Point Travelodge in one of the rooms overlooking the Brisbane river. The view from the balcony is spectacular and there is no finer place to eat breakfast and read the morning paper. Being close to the Gabba, it makes an ideal headquarters in Brisbane. This first visit to Brisbane was mercifully uneventful and simply revealed what most people had guessed, which was that without Imran Pakistan's bowling would be sadly inadequate. While we were flexing our muscles in Brisbane the summer was given a belligerent start by Dennis Lillee's comment after he had accepted the vice-captaincy of Western Australia. He was interviewed by Bob Maumill on Radio 6PR in Perth and was asked if this meant that he had patched up his differences with Kim Hughes who was the captain of the state team. 'Just because I have a drink with a bloke in the bar, it doesn't mean I am showing my sexual preference,' came the measured reply.

The Kangaroo Point Travelodge always reminds me of the time when in December 1968 on my first tour of Australia I became a temporary honorary member of the Queensland drug squad for a few hours one evening. Jack Lynchwaite, the head detective in the squad, came round to the Travelodge after the close of play one day to have a drink with Keith Butler who wrote cricket for the *Adelaide Advertiser*. He arrived with his two offsiders and I joined them all for a drink. After a while they had to go back on duty and Jack suggested to Keith and I that we might like to join them and see a bit of action.

It was too good an opportunity to miss and we piled into the back of a squad car. Jack now called up the station on the two-way radio and I was very disappointed when he was told that there was nothing on and that he had better go and have something to eat. We drove to the Breakfast Creek Inn where we ate the most delicious steaks which were produced in double-quick time when the manager saw who we were. Jack was a formidable character. In his late forties, he was a tough, leathery little man of relatively few words but with a good sense of humour. He clearly commanded great respect wherever we went. He had an impressive reputation and had won awards for his bravery when he was stationed in the Gulf of Carpentaria and places don't come much tougher than that. We washed the steak down with some beer and then it was back on duty. To my great relief, business was hotting up and after a conversation with headquarters on the radio, we were speeding towards an assignation. On the way, Jack asked me if I had noticed many Aborigines in Brisbane. I said I hadn't.

'You don't know where to look,' he smiled back at me.

We pulled up outside a sizeable pub which was some way from being the smartest I have ever seen. We pushed our way in, the three policemen first with Keith and I bringing up the rear and we found ourselves in an enormous barrack-like room which was full of Aborigines. The atmosphere was like thick fog and the noise deafening, but as soon as Jack was through the door an extraordinary silence descended on the room and hundreds of eyes were fixed on the five of us as we made our way to an empty table which had appeared as if by magic and glasses of beer were put in front of us. The three policemen talked amongst themselves and although I could not hear what was being said, they appeared to be talking about people who were wanted for questioning. Then, suddenly, Jack saw something for he stopped in mid-sentence and quietly said something to his colleagues who looked over towards the other side of the room. One of them then produced a photograph from his inside pocket and they were obviously in agreement that this was the person. After another word from Jack, the other two got up and began to thread their way through the tables towards the other side of the room watched in a menacing silence by every occupant. Then Jack spoke to Keith and I.

'There is someone over there we want. If there's any trouble go and stand by the door.'

There was none, which was a trifle disappointing, and the two returned with an Aborigine girl who must have been in her early twenties. We all went to the car and she sat in the front seat between Jack and the driver.

'You in trouble again?' Jack asked her.

'I was only let out of prison yesterday,' came the somewhat chilling reply. Apparently, she was wanted at the station for questioning and Jack told her that if she was a good girl and told the truth nothing would happen to her. They took her into the station and left her and then we were on our way again.

Unfortunately this was the last of the action and after a tour of a number of other Aborigine drinking haunts before closing time, we pulled up outside a small pub to have a drink ourselves after Jack had signed off over the radio. Before long we were joined inside by Ray Lindwall who owns a flower shop in Brisbane and conversation quickly turned from drugs to cricket. It was hot and after a while one of the detectives began to take off his jacket and then stopped when he was half out of it as if he had suddenly remembered something. But by then I had seen the black strap and the bulge of the shoulder holster, an extra piece of colour I enjoyed. It was well past midnight by the time we returned to Kangaroo Point and Jack left Keith and I with four Bowen mangoes each which he had brought back with him when he returned from North Queensland only the day before. I have enjoyed Bowen mangoes more than any other I have eaten and these were superb and so full of juice that the only practical way of eating them was standing naked in the bath. It had been an interesting evening and I found Jack a delightfully rich character. I was very sad to hear from the former Test match umpire Lou Rowan, who was also a detective in the drug squad, on one of my visits to Brisbane in 1983/ 84 that Jack had left the force.

Pakistan's bowling did not improve on the journey west. They drew with Queensland and then, in his first game, Abdul Qadir raised a nervous quiver among Australian batsmen as he spun South Australia to defeat with his leg breaks and googlies. My own best moment on that visit to Adelaide came when I bumped into Len Evans, Australia's leading wine authority, in the lift at the Hilton and he persuaded me to help him dispose of two bottles of Bollinger in his suite. The Pakistanis were brought back to reality in Perth when they were comfortably beaten by Western Australia. By then, they knew for sure that Imran would be unable to play in the first two Test matches. It was now clear that they desperately needed the services of Sarfraz Nawaz. But when he had been left out of the party to tour India he had publicly criticized the selectors and had been suspended by the Pakistan Board for six months. Imran and Sarfraz were friends and when I had written a piece from Brisbane saying then that they needed Sarfraz, Imran had told me that he hoped that and other pieces might prompt the authorities at home to change their minds, although Intikhab, the manager, was adamant that Sarfraz would not be coming. While we were in Adelaide, news came through that the suspension had been lifted and we awaited further developments. Sarfraz himself had been tracked down at home and in an interview with Ken Cunningham for Radio 5DN in Adelaide he had said that he would be there in time for the Third Test. He apparently knew more than anyone else. Our stay in Adelaide saw the arrival of the erstwhile captain, Zaheer Abbas. He had not come to Australia with the rest of the party for 'family reasons' which were more likely to have been umbrage for having been replaced. As it was, he wasted no time in telling a female journalist in Adelaide that he would soon be reappointed as the official captain of the tour. Clearly events were moving fast in Pakistan or at any rate in Karachi, which is Zaheer's home.

This was Rod Marsh's testimonial year and two days before the First Test a huge dinner for nearly 600 was held at the Perth-Sheraton where until recently the sales side of things had been presided over by that great cricket supporter Leon Larkin, whom the Sheraton group have now spirited away to Sydney where he continues to dispense extravagant hospitality to cricketers at the Sheraton-Wentworth. The organizers of the evening must have been hoping that by the time the dinner took place, in Marsh's home city, he would be the official captain of Australia. When I arrived in the country, it appeared that Marsh was the favourite to get the job, but strong lobbying had been going on and support for Kim Hughes had increased. The final decision was taken by the Australian Cricket Board. The day after the decision had been made, the Pakistanis were playing a one-day game against a country XI at Northiam and Hughes drove up to watch the game. Soon after he arrived he had the job of reading out to the assembled press the Australian squad for the First Test. Looking as though he was about to announce his own execution, he read the names in alphabetical order and after reading out 'Hughes', he added in the same monotone, 'captain'. So those of us who spoke that evening at the Sheraton in praise of Marsh had to be content to honour a great Australian wicket-keeper/batsman. Ian Chappell, Dennis Lillee and Mick Malone were three former team mates of Marsh's who spoke and it was a most enjoyable evening. Things got a little hotter at Marsh's dinner at the Sheraton-Wentworth in Sydney, but that was early in February and we were now in mid-November.

My own Australian summers find me glued more or less permanently to a telephone for four months. I produce a daily offering for *The Australian*, the only national daily in the country, and they allow me to tread my own path in any direction I like. Phil Wilkins was their chief cricket writer although he has now been succeeded by Terry Brindle, and I write a daily column. In addition to this, I work for a succession of commercial radio stations throughout the country. To know which is which and where they are to be found, one needs to be a qualified code breaker. In Sydney I belong to 2UE, in Melbourne it was 3UZ, and now 3AW, in Adelaide I work for 5DN and in Perth I am with 6PR. At times I have worked for 4BC and 4KQ in Brisbane. For UE, PR and UZ I do short reports for their news bulletins every hour on the hour from my telephone in the press box. I do a different report for each station and they are recorded just before the hour and then used in the news bulletin. For the last five minutes in every hour it is frenetic action. It is all quite an exercise in both vocal and physical gymnastics. I sign off at the end of every report with, 'This is Henry Blofeld for 6PR' or whatever the station is that I am talking to. Sometimes I forget where I am, occasionally who I am and more often I cannot remember who I am talking to. In the space of those five minutes I have to dial the three stations and do three reports of about 45 seconds off the top of my head. Of course, if I get cut off or someone in the studio works the recorder wrong it becomes a major crisis because the last call can get squeezed out. Still, it is a lot of fun and so far not enough people have complained to get me taken off the air. Although I had been doing reports at each interval during the state games, my radio output did not move into top gear until the Test series began in Perth.

Perth is also the scene of another minor involvement I have in Australia. In the last few years, indoor cricket has, rather surprisingly, swept through Australia. Surprisingly because it is a country with such a marvellous outdoor climate that one would have thought that there would have been no great support for any attempt to take a form of the game indoors. Indoor Cricket Arenas is the company which has pioneered the game throughout Australia and had its headquarters at a huge indoor sporting complex called Lords in the Perth suburb of Subiaco before moving to Melbourne. ICA was the brainchild of Paul Hanna who watched it grow from one two-court centre in Perth to more than seventy centres through the country with more going up all the time. The company, which is owned by Kevin Bain and Gary Harley at the time of writing, is at present bringing the game to England where the climate is at any rate more suitable.

It is played in a net which is thirty metres long and eleven metres across. There are eight players a side and each side bowls sixteen eight-ball overs. The batsmen bat in pairs and each pair faces four overs. Every member of the fielding side has to bowl two overs and runs are scored by hitting the ball into different areas of the side netting for which respectively the batsmen get one, two, four or six. Runs are also scored by running between the wickets in the normal way. Every time a batsman is out five runs are deducted from the side's score. A game lasts for exactly an hour and a half and the action is non-stop and exciting. It is a marvellous game in its own right and in Australia getting on for 100,000 people play. I am sure it has a big future.

When I was in Perth, the city was still vigorously hugging itself after *Australia II*'s incredible victory in the America's Cup. The singularly ugly cup was on view in the museum and as *Australia II* was still on the way home there was nothing much to see at the Royal Perth Yacht

Club where we all assembled one evening before the Test for a bar-
becue. By then, the new chairman of the Australian Cricket Board,
Fred Bennett, had spoken to the Australian players about the loyalty
he expected them to show to Hughes who was known not to be the
choice of all the players as captain. It was an unusual step for the
chairman to take, but it should have helped clear the air and also have
shown the players that Bennett was intending to be a chairman who
led from the front. It was ironical that the very next day at this party
at the Royal Perth Yacht Club a lengthy and extremely heated argument took place at a considerable decibel level between Kim Hughes
and Rod Marsh. The exchanges were fierce and it was all visible and
audible to the entire company which included Fred Bennett himself.

The first Test was played on a grassy pitch with enough bounce to
give batsmen who had just come from India's lifeless pitches recurring
nightmares, and the game was therefore heavily tilted in Australia's
favour. Zaheer as the official vice-captain was in charge of Pakistan in
Imran's absence and when he won the toss he must have been scared
stiff at what he saw and decided to field first. Pakistan's own seam
bowlers were not fast or accurate enough to make use of the conditions
and Abdul Qadir, who insisted on bowling round the wicket at Australia's phalanx of left handers, bowled badly. Wayne Phillips made
159 in his first Test innings and must have been grateful to have played
it against such a limited attack. Of course, batsmen are not able to
choose the bowlers they will bat against in their first Test. If they
could, the record books would read very differently. Phillips was lucky,
but he took his chance well. There was also a good hundred from
Graham Yallop who never allowed Abdul Qadir to settle down.

Pakistan were then blasted out in a rush, principally by Carl Rackemann and Rodney Hogg although both Dennis Lillee and Geoff Lawson had their moments. By no means all Pakistan's batsmen relished
the fight against the quick stuff and in truth it was hard to blame
them. Maurice Leyland, the old Yorkshire and England batsman, once
said, 'None of us likes the short stuff, but some of us shows it more
than others.' Pakistan were short on disguise. The one notable exception was Qasim Omar, the smallest player on either side, who took
everything that came to him and batted for two and a half hours,
making 48 in the first innings; he followed this with 65 in the second.
In the first innings in particular he was hit all over the body as he
moved unflinchingly into line. After he had been brilliantly caught by
Yallop in the gully, he lay on the massage table in the dressing room

while the Pakistan physiotherapist put ice packs on the worst bruises. Five were in place and as he approached with the sixth, Omar looked at him with a broad smile on his face and said, 'Wouldn't it be better if I got into the fridge.' In spite of Qasim Omar, Australia won by an innings and nine runs.

There is no aeroplane journey I enjoy less in the whole year than the 'red-eye special' from Perth to Sydney. It leaves Perth at around midnight, our watches go forward two hours and we get to Melbourne sometime after five in the morning. We then have to stagger off the aeroplane, bleary-eyed, and slump onto an airport bench until it is time for the connecting flight to Sydney at eight o'clock. All I want to do when I eventually get to Sydney is to spend the rest of the day in bed in a state of total exhaustion.

Pakistan against New South Wales was never likely to be a fixture which would quicken many pulses and after the disappointing Test match in Perth, hardly anyone turned up to watch at the Sydney Cricket Ground. While the cricket was little more than an academic exercise, it provided a last chance to watch Rick McCosker play the late cut, nowadays such an unfashionable stroke, in his last season before retiring. Dirk Wellham, NSW's new captain, also busied about calling for runs with screams and yells which suggested he might have been opening the batting for Yorkshire. He has fallen out of favour since scoring that hundred at the Oval in 1981 in his first Test match. This game saw the vast new electronic scoreboard on the Hill in action for the first time. While some traditionalists may not approve of these inventions, I found it easy to follow and rather exciting. The Sydney scoreboard was Mitsubishi Mark II compared to Melbourne's Mitsubishi Mark I, but I doubt if Japan's entry into big cricket will ever go beyond commercial electronics. Anyway, the lovely blonde Anna, who had worked the computer in the Melbourne scoreboard, had travelled up to Sydney to make sure this one had a smooth start.

While the match meandered on, I ran into Australia's leading actress, Kate Fitzpatrick, who, on a whim of David Hill's, had just become Channel Nine's newest commentator and she was to start the following week in the Second Test in Brisbane. She was sitting in the pavilion brushing up on her leg breaks and googlies. She was also conducting a long interview with Imran Khan for her column in the *Sydney Morning Herald*. She produced a most interesting piece which really caught the flavour of her victim. On the Saturday and Sunday the cricket had to bear competition from the warming-up noises which were going on at the Showground in preparation for David Bowie's two concerts. While the sound system was experimented with, various groups were rehearsing and when the volume was turned up it was sheer agony. The concerts began in the early evening after the close of play and on leaving the SCG the cricket supporters had to fight their way through a vastly different audience which was arriving for David Bowie who I met briefly on the Saturday evening.

I was about to go up to bed round about midnight when I came across Imran Khan in the lobby of the Sheraton-Wentworth. He asked me if I would like to come with him to David Bowie's after-concert party at the Sebel Town House. We hailed a taxi and as Imran was able to drop the right names we managed to fight our way through an impressive security network and shot up in the lift to the penthouse suite. On arrival our credentials were again put to the test before we were allowed in and given a drink. There were a fair number of teeny-boppers and a variety of others including Paul Dainty who had set the tour up. After a while, the great man himself wandered past all on his own and I am ashamed to say that I went up and introduced myself and gave him a fearful ear-bashing for about five minutes. The poor chap looked slightly bemused and then moved on. So did Imran and I.

5
On Board the Cricket Caravan

A visit to his doctor in Sydney had put off Imran's impending return
for a while longer and there was a definite uneasiness in the ranks of
the Pakistanis when they arrived in Brisbane three days before the
Second Test. The man I felt most sorry for apart from Imran was their
urbane and avuncular manager, Intikhab Alam, who in his day had
himself been no mean purveyor of leg breaks. He is the most genial of
men and I find it difficult to think of anyone less suited to coping with
the politically inspired upheavals which began in Brisbane. He spent
much of his time denying a succession of rumours as forcibly and as
convincingly as he could, but succeeded only in sounding apologetic
and less than convincing.

Intikhab began the Pakistanis' first day in Brisbane by denying, for
him most emphatically, that the tour management had any intention
of sending for Sarfraz as a reinforcement. This was followed by a telex
message and a telephone call from the secretary of the Pakistan Cricket
Board in Pakistan saying that from now on Zaheer Abbas was the
official captain of the party in Australia. As soon as Zaheer heard the
news he decided that as the party in Australia was Imran's and not his
own, wholesale reinforcements were needed. As a result before the day
had ended Intikhab found himself on the telephone to Pakistan asking
for Sarfraz and Salim Malik to be sent out soonest. Meanwhile Zaheer
was photographed being 'chaired' by his players and it was all over
the next day's papers. That night Zaheer went to bed as the new
commander-in-chief while Imran said that he was prepared to play
under anyone. The next morning Intikhab was still anxious for con-
firmation of Zaheer's appointment and eventually tracked down Air
Marshal Nur Khan, the president of the Board of Control, in London.

We were told that Nur Khan instantly reappointed Imran. But when I was in Pakistan with the England side the following March, I was told that Zaheer had been called by his supporters in Karachi, who included the deposed chairman of the selectors Asib Hasan, and told that as this was not his team he must refuse the captaincy. Imran was thus reinstated.

It was almost impossible to follow what was happening on the spot in Brisbane and it was most certainly a long way from the ideal build-up to a crucial Test match for the Pakistanis. The pattern of the first match was faithfully repeated except this time Zaheer decided to bat when he won the toss and Pakistan were bowled out for 156 on a pitch which again helped Australia's fast bowlers. Greg Chappell then made 150 not out and saw Australia to a lead of 353, but on the last day Pakistan were saved by a thunderstorm which was a fairly modest affair compared to Brisbane's normal standards. By then Australia's fast bowlers had taken three wickets. So the Pakistanis departed for Melbourne with a small measure of confidence, for not only had they escaped defeat, but also Sarfraz, who had been eventually tracked down in Bombay, would be in Melbourne to meet them.

No account of a Test at the Gabba is ever complete without a vote of thanks to those who each day produce for the media baskets of delicious fresh fruit which is spread out on tables behind the commentary boxes. Throughout the match, Lou Rowan, in his usual excellent form, dispenses lethal gin and tonics in the Brisbane Cricket Ground Trust offices. One day during the Second Test he showed me the photograph of his former colleague, Col Egar, with his arm outstretched at square leg after calling Ian Meckiff for throwing in the First Test against South Africa at the Gabba in 1963/64. Lou Rowan's office is a great meeting place and Ray Lindwall, Peter Burge, Alan McGilvray, members of the Australian Cricket Board and the Test selectors all enjoy those excellent drinks. My only other adventure in Brisbane was an excellent dinner with a feature writer on *The Australian*, Liz Johnston, who had been asked by the editor to write a piece about me. The food was good, the champagne excellent and she sent me up no more than I deserved. On one day of the Test I ran into Ray Ham who had bought the franchise for Indoor Cricket Arenas in Queensland and decided to organize a Henry Blofeld Cup to be played for between the four centres so far open and to hold the final on my return visit to Brisbane for the two one-day games in January. Then it was on to Melbourne.

It was good to be back at the Windsor Hotel which had for so many years been the traditional home for cricketers in the city and which is owned nowadays by the Oberoi Group. It had just emerged from a fallow period and was almost at the end of a thirteen million dollar facelift. The rooms had all been done up and were excellent and my only complaint was that in the Grill Room they would serve Tasmanian and not Sydney oysters, and probably in the main restaurant too. The Cricketers Bar was in full swing although a good deal of the memorabilia which lined the walls had disappeared down Collins Street to the Hotel Australia with the former manager Alan Carruthers. The Windsor has always had a huge lounge where drinks and buffet meals are served and which has a splendid grand piano in the middle. It is all delightfully formal and jeans are most definitely not allowed. One day I went in wearing what I considered to be a smart pair of blue Italian trousers. A waitress sprung out at me and told me that I could not come in wearing jeans. I explained rather testily that far from being jeans they were distinctly upmarket. I got nowhere and rather disgruntled I had to go and change and re-emerged wearing a pair of trousers which were legal but far less elegant. It was sad to hear that Len, the old head porter, had had a stroke a week or so before I arrived in Melbourne.

When Imran had been reinstated he agreed that Sarfraz should join the side, but Salim Malik's arrival was delayed. Sarfraz was waiting for his colleagues in Melbourne and proceeded to bowl a great many overs against Victoria without suggesting that he was going to get many people out. Ray Bright, Victoria's captain, continued their first innings until half an hour after tea on the second day and then Pakistan had a bit of a scramble to avoid the follow on but went on to win the match when Mudassar and Javed hit fine hundreds on the last day. It was Mudassar's second hundred of the match. In all the matches at the MCG in 1983/4, I joined the Radio 3UZ commentary team for the ball-by-ball commentary with Ian Meckiff, the former Australian fast bowler whose Test career was ended that day by Col Egar at Brisbane, Ray Jordon, the old Victorian wicket-keeper who toured South Africa in 1969/70 without getting a Test cap, and John McKinnon. It is to say the least a light-hearted form of commentary and with Ray Jordon, nicknamed 'Slug', it could hardly be anything else for he never stops making the most engagingly outrageous remarks. It is difficult for anyone to take offence for it is all done with great humour. At times he makes it almost impossible for the other commentators for he reduces them to hopeless laughter. The worst moment of all came during one of the one-day matches towards the end of the season when Ray and John were discussing someone's secretary who was obviously far from plain. After a while Ray turned to John and said on the air, 'You been there?' It was a moment or two before order was restored.

When I arrived at the Hilton in the middle of Adelaide, I found a bright red express carrier envelope waiting for me with the galley proofs of *Wine, Women and Wickets* which kept me busy that evening and I was able to shuttle them back to Sydney the next day. This is the point at which I get slightly cold feet about a book for it has now passed the point of no return. The Pakistanis had something of a surprise when they arrived in Adelaide for they found Salim Malik awaiting them. Imran had seen his doctor on another trip to Sydney and now insisted that he would play in the last two Tests as a batsman. Twelve months earlier in Adelaide, England's captain, Bob Willis, had as a result of a consensus decision elected to field first when he won the toss. It was one of the outstanding acts of lunacy since Test cricket was invented and England lost the match with plenty to spare. Now, with both their new arrivals in the side, Zaheer lost the toss and Pakistan had a dreadful first day in the field. Kepler Wessels and Allan Border both made big scores, two crucial catches were dropped, and there appeared to be no thought or plan of action about the entire performance. There was depressingly little challenge about any of Pakistan's cricket.

It could hardly have been a worse first day, but what went on that evening in the hotel may never be revealed. Sarfraz, for sure, spoke his mind in the strongest possible terms and probably directed most of his criticism at Zaheer whose captaincy had been almost non-existent. He had shown no imagination and even a reluctance to make the obvious moves. The result of all this behind-the-scenes activity was that Pakistan were a completely different side the next day. They were sharper and more purposeful and to keep Australia to 465 was no mean achievement. On the field Sarfraz was the inspiration and he bowled well without any luck. Even on the docile Adelaide pitch, where the ball seldom came through above waist height, Australia's fast bowlers were too much for Mudassar. When he was out Qasim Omar took his place and proceeded to take control with a marvellous display of driving against all the fast bowlers. He and Mohsin put on 233 for the second wicket. At lunch on the third day Qasim Omar was 94 not out and obviously highly nervous at the thought of his approaching hundred. As he came off the field he was descended upon by masses of small boys for his autograph. Although he must have longed for the calm of the pavilion, he took off his gloves, put his bat down on a bench and signed every autograph book which was put in front of him, which delayed his lunch for almost fifteen minutes. I cannot think of another Test cricketer who would have bothered. It was a little sad but maybe a sign of the times that when I told this story to a current Australian Test cricketer who was not playing in the match, his immediate answer was, 'I suppose that makes him a great player.'

Soon after the interval Omar square drove left-arm spinner Tom Hogan for four and he jumped around punching the air in his delight at reaching the hundred everyone in Australia was willing him to get. The public had taken hugely to this irresistible character and his guts and indomitable cheerfulness. When Omar had reached 52 he had played forward to Hogan and had been given out caught off bat and pad by Wessels at forward short leg, but Wessels had immediately indicated that the ball had bounced before going into his hands and recalled Omar. Omar's second reaction after reaching his hundred had been to shake Wessels' hand. He had made 113 when he played forward to Lillee and was caught behind while Mohsin went on to reach 149 and Pakistan were finally taken to 624 by Javed Miandad who made 131 and newcomer Salim Malik who contributed a handsome 77. This gave Pakistan a lead of 159 and Abdul Qadir the chance to confuse Australia's batsmen. Again he did not bowl well, operating mostly round the wicket to the left handers, and Australia were saved by a fine aggressive hundred by Hughes who showed that for all the criticism he may attract as a captain, he is a batsman of the highest class.

When the game was over and the awards had been made, I noticed Abdul Qadir and Imran Khan talking earnestly to Richie Benaud who was one of the best leg spinners of all. I was sure that Qadir would be a wiser bowler after their conversation. He is anyway one of the most delightfully entertaining bowlers I have seen. It is as if he is walking on springs as he bounces up to the wicket to bowl. First, he spins himself a catch from right hand to left and is about three strides into his run when he transfers the ball back again; there then follows the lovely high action and the leg break, the top spinner or one of two googlies, and if he thinks he has troubled the batsman his arm comes over again after delivering the ball in a sort of victory twirl. He has an enormous amount of natural ability, but his main trouble is that he seems to be carried along on a bubble of enthusiasm which does not

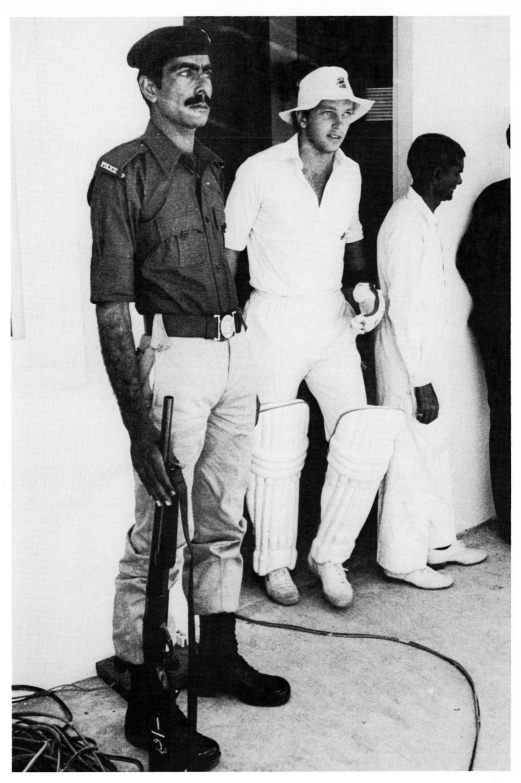

David Gower leaves the dressing room at Lahore in the Third Test, March 1984, and finds the moment more jolly than his grim-faced protector

The new face of cricket. The huge electronic scoreboard on the Hill at Sydney being used for the first time when Pakistan played New South Wales in November 1983

The old scoreboard has at last been retired except for Sheffield Shield matches and a distinguished group says farewell: Richie Benaud, Keith Miller, Arthur Morris, Brian Booth, Bobby Simpson and Neil Harvey

Yet another milestone. Greg Chappell has just passed Don Bradman's aggregate of runs in Test cricket in his final match in January 1984 against Pakistan

Pakistan's newest batting hero, Qasim Omar, never flinched once. Here he does his best to make up for his lack of inches against another Lillee bouncer in the 1983/84 series in Australia

Below The time has come to call it a day. During the Fifth Test against Pakistan in Sydney, Greg Chappell tells the media that this is the last one

Learie Constantine, out of retirement for a friendly match. He was undoubtedly the inspiration for future generations of West Indies players

Below The stress fracture to Imran Khan's left shin kept him out of the first three Tests against Australia in the 1983/84 series and effectively ruined Pakistan's chances. Here he receives treatment

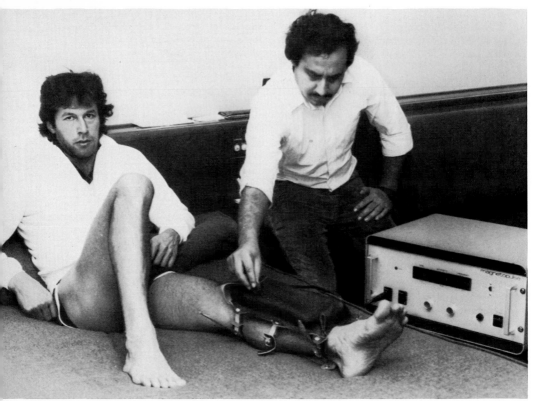

involve thinking too deeply about his art. This bubble can be pricked all too easily and when that happens he has nothing to fall back on. He does not try and work out a plan of campaign against a batsman, and attempt to sort out his strengths and weaknesses and to bowl accordingly. Instead, he tries to take a wicket every ball and he will show a new batsman all the weapons in his armoury in his first couple of overs at him. He uses the googly so much that it is no longer a surprise and in any event bowling round the wicket for much of the time lessens its effectiveness. If only he could learn to work on a new batsman, perhaps bowling him two overs of leg breaks before throwing in a googly to catch the batsman unawares, he would be a more formidable bowler. He has a wide repertoire but is tactically unaware.

The evidence of Pakistan's next few games suggested that Richie Benaud was warning him against using a forward short leg and a silly point on Australian pitches. These fielders may have picked up plenty of catches for him on the slow pitches of Pakistan, but in these first three Test matches in Australia they had not had a single chance off bat and pad. But with these two fielders up for the close catch, it meant that there were gaps elsewhere into which the batsman was able to push the ball for singles to get away from the strike if he was in trouble. No bowler can keep a batsman under pressure if he generously provides the means for him to get down to the other end. Another of Qadir's troubles was probably that he allowed himself to become easily depressed and was then unable to work out the value of all the different pieces of advice he was constantly being given.

I enjoy the Adelaide Test more than any other in the cricketing calendar. The Adelaide Oval is, along with Newlands in Cape Town and Queen's Park Oval, Port of Spain, one of the three most beautiful Test grounds in the world. For the Test, the lawns and tennis courts at the back of the members' stands are covered with marquees which dispense marvellous picnic lunches for those lucky enough to have been selected. Thomas Hardy, the winemakers from the Barossa Valley, pour their product suitably chilled in another tent, the ladies always seem to be about the most beautiful in the world and an Adelaide Test has the atmosphere of the most jolly cricketing garden party.

I watch the match from Radio 5DN's commentary box, which is perched at the back of the main stand, and sit beside that incorrigible enthusiast Ken Cunningham. Ken or KG as he is known to everyone in South Australia, has a highly interesting and entertaining daily sports programme in which he talks to sportsmen of the moment in any part of the world, and he also leads the station's commentary team for the cricket. He was himself a most useful batsman who played for the state for many years. I can think of no one I enjoy working with more, especially when he gets carried away by a fine piece of cricket – as long as it comes from an Australian or, even better, a South Australian. I always tell him he is as one-eyed as it is possible to be and during this Adelaide Test he produced two splendid comments. Lillee took a wicket and KG said 'and Lillee has the superb figures of 4/168' and a little later 'Pakistan are in the quite good position of 5/580.' I could not let him get away with those two. We seem to spend most of our time laughing while we are doing commentary and KG is a sucker for two of Brian Johnston's classics. When we had a streaker at the Adelaide Oval during the England Test in 1982/83, he jumped over the wooden paling fence as he came off the ground, causing us all to draw in our breath pretty sharply as he did not clear one of the spikes by much. I was able to say, as Brian had done at Lord's during a streaker's visit to the 1975 World Cup final, 'It's all right, the umpire hasn't signalled one short.' The other one comes when a batsman has played a slow innings and I have to read out his statistics. 'He hit nine fours, batted for 298 minutes and faced 203 balls, which is an awful lot of balls.'

There was another time at the Adelaide Oval when I said that if one side won a Test I would eat my hat. The next day a bowler hat made a magic appearance in the box which I was made to wear during my commentary spells. When, in the closing overs, it began to look as if I might after all have to eat it, Ian Chappell, who always joins our team, spent a lot of time deciding which part I should eat first. Mercifully the game ended in a draw and my digestive system was spared the ordeal. During this Test against Pakistan, Ian announced that he had just reached forty and sounded a bit gloomy. I sympathized with him and told him I knew just how he felt for I was still confidently expecting to be nineteen next birthday. 'The trouble with you Blowers,' he said, 'is that you act like it too.' It's all a good laugh and we are joined by a constant flow of past and present Test cricketers who come along to give us their views on what is happening. It is a splendid mixture.

After Adelaide the caravan descended, as it always does, on Hobart and we had the most delightful few days in Tasmania's capital. Imran Khan played his first game of the tour with limited success although

Pakistan defeated Tasmania on the charming ground in the Domain which overlooks Government House and the Derwent River. I had one excellent dinner at Mures in Battery Point which is the most delicious fish restaurant. I also made my usual rather heavy donation to the Croupiers' Benevolent Fund at the Wrest Point Casino. There was not much significance to the cricket and we all returned to Melbourne for the Christmas festivities and the Fourth Test with our batteries happily recharged. I would not miss those few days in Hobart for anything in the world.

Christmas Eve and Boxing Day passed off in a mild alcoholic haze. The Fourth Test then brought Pakistan another outside chance of victory, but once again on a slow pitch Abdul Qadir was unable to produce the goods. Mohsin Khan played a fine innings of 152 and Imran himself made 83, showing what a high-class batsman he is. If he had concentrated more on his batting earlier in his career he would have had figures to rank with any all-rounder. It was Imran who made sure that Pakistan scored enough runs to give their bowlers a chance. As it happened Graham Yallop batted magnificently and scored 268, demonstrating what an enigma he has become. His figures suggest he should surely have played more for Australia than he has. He does not have a particularly athletic build and he is not as graceful a stroke-maker as many left-handers, yet the sheer weight of runs he has scored in the last few years is solid enough proof of his ability. Yet Yallop has tended to pick and choose his opponents and a knee injury has constantly kept him out of engagements with the West Indies. Sometimes he has appeared to shirk the challenge.

He was principally responsible for taking Australia to a lead of 85 and when Lillee and Lawson took three Pakistan second innings wickets for 38 on the fourth evening, they were obviously going to struggle on the last day to avoid defeat. As it was, another determined innings by Imran saw the danger pass for Pakistan. This match saw the introduction of off spinner Greg Matthews to Test cricket and he looked a better batsman than bowler. He made an attractive 75 at the end of Australia's innings and as an individual he is not short of confidence. The story has it that when he was stopped from going into the Australian dressing room by the attendant at the MCG, he produced his credentials and then added, 'You had better get used to my face as I am going to be around for a long time.' He may have been rather too optimistic.

We had a lot of fun in the Radio 3UZ commentary box, one of six new boxes built above the new press box at the MCG. We were without Ian Meckiff who was on his annual visit to the New South Wales Victorian border where, judging from his stories on his return, he spent as much time improving the profits of the local brewery as he did trying to catch the fish which he claimed to be his main objective. We were joined in his place by Jackie Potter, a former captain of Victoria whose comments were pithy and to the point if less ebullient than Ray Jordon's. The most amusing commentary box story of the match came from the 3AW box which houses our then rivals, whose team I was to join in 1984/5. Their commentators, led by Harry Beitzel, had evolved a way of describing the game by using the face of the clock to indicate fielding positions rather than using the normal names. The batsman is at twelve o'clock, cover point at nine o'clock and square leg at three o'clock, and so on. The idea presumably is not to confuse the layman with the names of fielding positions he may not understand. The result is that magnificent drives go flashing to the boundary at half-past seven or half-past five. Harry did all the commentary and I don't know how he kept it up all day. On one occasion in this match he had gone into ecstasies about a fine catch by an Australian at half-past six. Then he corrected himself and said that it was closer to a quarter-past six before handing back to the studio for the news. The announcer came in saying how marvellous it was to hear about that catch at a quarter-past six. He continued, 'And now I'm going to read you the deep fine leg news.' In 1984/5 we had returned to the traditional field placings.

6
Cricket and Other Distractions

It was some time now since the Pakistan authorities at home had provided us with any good copy. There had been a slight ripple when, after the Hobart match, their fast-medium bowler, Atiq-ur-Rahman, who had bowled just thirty overs in the first two games of the tour and had not played since, was sent back to Pakistan. The tour committee felt that he would be better off playing cricket at home rather than following the side round in Australia where he would not play another game. I could not help feeling very sorry for the guy, who must have arrived in Australia with high hopes, when I saw him traipse off to the international departure lounge at Melbourne Airport. But they made up for this rather disappointing lack of incident during the Fourth Test in Melbourne when Imran decided that he wanted the services of left-arm spinner Iqbal Qasim for the Fifth Test in Sydney. The request went back to Pakistan where the new chairman of the selectors was Ijaz Butt, who looks after the Lahore Cricket Assocation and managed the Pakistan side which toured Australia in 1981/82. By the time the team had reached Sydney, word had come back from Lahore, after a slight delay, that Iqbal Qasim was not being sent to Australia for he would not arrive in Sydney in time for the first ball. The President of the Pakistan Board of Control, Air Marshal Nur Khan, was with the players in Australia and I would think that he reacted to the news in a pretty tight-lipped fashion. Imran and manager Intikhab certainly seemed less than enchanted. It was about now that rumours began to circulate that the reserve wicker-keeper, Ashraf Ali, would be catching an early aeroplane home. His finest hour had come, strangely enough, with a remarkable catch on the deep-square-leg boundary against South Australia in the second game of the tour when he was fielding as a substitute. It was the catch which effectively stopped David Hookes's chances of batting his way into the Test series.

If anything, the New Year celebrations were more alcoholic than the Christmas festivities. On New Year's Eve I was invited by Leon Larkin to a magnificent dinner party at the Sheraton-Wentworth and I knew as soon as I saw the invitation that it would be one of those evenings which would produce something in excess of a five-aspirin hangover which would mock at large doses of vitamin B. As a result, New Year's Day turned out to be one of those mornings of which the memory is, to say the least, a trifle sketchy. I did remember that sitting on my right hand at dinner was Bob Radford, the unfailingly affable secretary of the New South Wales Cricket Association. He was wearing a black plastic top hat throughout – I probably was too for we had all found one at our places – and he firmly assured me that Test cricket had had it. I begged to differ in no less forceful terms, but it was sad to hear someone so closely involved with cricket administration in Australia feeling that this was so.

At the moment, one-day internationals are drawing much bigger crowds than the Test matches, especially during a series where the result is not particularly close. My own feeling is that there will always be room for both types of the game and that Test cricket will at least pay for itself and rather more than that when England or the West Indies are Australia's opponents. Beating the Poms is a national pastime in Australia and even if England should lose every Test the crowds will go on rising. I believe too that the one-day internationals, which attract a new audience to the game, are helped by the direct and immediate comparison with the longer-drawn-out Test cricket. The Australians, in particular, love cocking a snoop at tradition and in a sense by coming to watch one-day cricket they are having a go at Test cricket. If the immediate comparison between the two types of the game was not so readily available, I am not sure that one-day cricket would benefit so strongly from the them-and-us situation which now exists. Also I think that the Australian public would quickly become fed up with it all if, instead of 25 days of Test cricket and 18 one-day games – the present mixture – they had to suffer 43 one-day affairs each year.

Bob Radford's point was heavily underlined when Australia played the West Indies at the SCG in one of the preliminary matches in 1983/84 for the Benson & Hedges World Series Cup under the floodlights and it was a sell-out. Radford sent a message up to me in the press-box to say that he had had to ring round all the local radio stations asking them to tell people not to turn up unless they had a ticket and that he had never had to do that even for one day's play in a Test match. If my memory serves me right he went on at dinner that night to forecast the extinction of Test cricket in ten years, but under pressure he qualified this by adding 'in Australia'. There is no doubt though that one-day international cricket is what makes Australia's ambitious annual international programme financially viable. It is the icing on the cake, but take away the cake and you may find that the icing will not be spread quite so thick.

The Fifth Test was won, predictably enough, by Australia by the convincing margin of ten wickets which gave them the series by two matches to nil. Long after the details of the match have been forgotten, it will be remembered as the last occasion on which Greg Chappell, Dennis Lillee and Rod Marsh played together for Australia. For this reason I have decided to describe the match in full in the next chapter. Appropriately all three of them made telling contributions to Australia's victory in a game which brought to an end a remarkable era in Australian cricket. Chappell and Lillee both retired from international cricket after this match while Marsh hung on until the end of the one-day competition.

Sydney in the New Year saw Kate Fitzpatrick return from the commentators' box to the theatre. She opened at the Opera House in a play called *Insignificance* in which she played the part of Marilyn Monroe to whom she was made up to bear an astonishing resemblance. It was a conversation piece between Monroe, Albert Einstein, Senator McCarthy and Joe Dimaggio. Kate was superb and made what I found really rather a heavy play come to life. While Sydney without the Harbour Bridge or the Opera House is unthinkable, Sydney without Diana Fisher or Fishpots would be just as impossible. Fishpots is Sydney's answer to Nigel Dempster and William Hickey with a suspicion of Jennifer's Diary thrown in and most definitely shaken and not stirred. If there are any gossip columns in Australia not written by Fishpots, their stories seem almost invariably to be about her. She is unique. I have never come across anyone who is half as kind and so extraordinarily generous. The moment she knows a friend is in Sydney, she is on the telephone arranging a party. If it is an England cricket tour she enlists the help of Peter Doyle who owns Sydney's finest fish restaurant in Watson's Bay. Peter lays on his considerable boat and we, the journalists, spend an unforgettable morning cruising round the harbour drinking delicious white wine and scoffing platefuls of that morning's catch of prawns. Peter is also not averse to giving a useful lesson in prawnsmanship. 'Twist off the head. Then, finger and thumb pressed together halfway down the body. Peel off the top half of the shell in one go and now squeeze the prawn out of the bottom half of the shell and there it is.' Simple. And delicious too at the end of it. After hugging the shore of the Eastern Suburbs while Peter gives us the lowdown on the multi-millionaires who own the waterside houses and discusses the merits of the helicopters perched on several of the lawns, we turn round up by the Opera House. Then, we go down towards the Heads past Sydney's first nudist beach on the right, although whenever I have seen it from Peter's boat it has always appeared to be men-only day which is most disappointing. We always end up at Peter's restaurant at Watson's Bay for the most superbly boozy and delicious lunch. Fishpots flashes away like mad throughout the day with her newest camera and most of us appear in one of her many columns over the next week or two. Then, on one day of the Test match she always turns up at the Sydney Cricket Ground with the ultimate in picnic lunches which she dispenses on the small stand on the number two ground. As far as I am concerned Fishpots is the patron saint of gossip columnists and she had her finest hour on the night that *Wine, Women and Wickets* was launched in Sydney. Elton John had most inconsiderately decided to get married at almost exactly the same time. Fishpots took both events in her stride. In fact, she came to the launch party at the Sheraton-Wentworth before buzzing off to the church in King's Cross. She was back to have dinner with us at Pronto's in Double Bay and then returned to the Sebel Town House and Elton John's reception, but we are getting slightly ahead of ourselves. Fishpots is also called Bubbles and she in turn calls everyone Darling, and I doubt you would ever pick her as a daughter-in-law of Lord Fisher, the former Archbishop of Canterbury.

7

Farewell Test

It was extraordinary that the series had still not been decided when Australia and Pakistan came to Sydney for the Fifth Test, but Australia's victory in the First in Perth had been the only definite result in the first four matches. From a logical point of view it was still just as impossible to give Pakistan a realistic chance of victory. But then, there was always the chance that Abdul Qadir might at the end get it right. On the evidence of the series so far, this could be no more than a pious hope for the Pakistanis. They played the side which had drawn the Fourth Test in Melbourne while Australia brought back Rodney Hogg who was fit again, in place of John Maguire who bowls fast medium and bats a bit.

It was a wet Monday morning and for some time it did not look as if there would be any play that day. The rain stopped around lunchtime and after a noisy but effective visit by the Channel Nine helicopter which hovered low over the wettest patches so that the down-draught could dry them out, the umpires decided that play could start at four o'clock. Kim Hughes won the toss for Australia and put Pakistan in to bat on a pitch which was tinged with green and was likely to help his faster bowlers. The rules decreed that at least nineteen overs would have to be bowled that evening and Pakistan's opening pair of Mudassar and Mohsin will not have relished the prospect of batting against Dennis Lillee, Geoff Lawson and Hogg. They were soon looking distinctly uneasy and it came as no surprise when in the seventh over Mohsin drove at Lillee and was caught by Allan Border at second slip. Little Qasim Omar took his place and edged his first ball through the slips along the ground for four. Indeed every ball could have been the last for either batsman. There is no more difficult time for batsmen than a short spell of cricket like this. There is no time to settle in, with so few overs to bowl the bowlers can give everything, and although playable the conditions are distinctly unfriendly. All they dare try and do is defend, which of course hands over the initiative to the bowlers. Just before the close Pakistan lost Qasim Omar too. He fenced at a shorter one from Lillee and Border threw himself to his left at second slip and held a remarkable two-handed catch. Omar departed a forlorn figure, looking in his dejection even smaller than his five foot four. On the other hand Lillee, much larger than life, trumpeted down the pitch in unbridled delight at taking his 349th Test wicket. That lovely smooth approach, the beautiful action and the control were all still there. By the close of play Pakistan had limped to 61/2.

The weather had mended its ways the next morning and although Australia's bowlers worked their way systematically through the Pakistan batting order, the rumours which had begun before the start of play claimed most attention – from the media at any rate. Apparently Greg Chappell was going to announce his retirement after the close of play and that was the day's story. For a moment it seemed extraordinary that he could even contemplate retirement for there he was in the slips where he has always been and looking no different, certainly not any older. Suddenly it ceased to be a Test match and became a nostalgic finale.

Mechanically, I noted the fall of the wickets. Abdul Qadir, the night-watchman, steered Lawson to Hughes at third slip. That was 67/3. One run later Mudassar fished for a wide one and Marsh took off yet again in a flashing dive towards the slips, yet this one somehow got away. Mudassar was dropped by Border at second slip soon afterwards. He and Javed Miandad took the score to 131 when Javed went back and pulled Greg Matthews powerfully to mid wicket without getting right on top of the ball and Lillee held a low, hard catch. It was time for more congratulations and at lunch Pakistan were 139/4.

Immediately afterwards the first of several semi-miraculous occurrences which made this match so memorable took place. Chappell came into this Test with 119 catches to his credit and needed one to equal and two to beat Colin Cowdrey's record of 120. Lawson ran in to bowl to Mudassar who played back, the ball found the edge and there was Chappell outwardly unconcerned at second slip throwing up his 120th catch. Mudassar's 84 had been his biggest innings in this series. Like so many batsmen before him, he was unable to come to terms with the steeper bounce on Australian pitches. Imran hooked and skied

Lawson to mid wicket before Salim Malik, a wonderfully talented young player, and Zaheer Abbas, whose nerve against the quick bowlers is not what it used to be, put on 96 entertaining runs. Then Salim hooked at Lawson and Lillee held the skier. When thirteen runs later Sarfraz played forward and was lbw, Lillee had taken his 350th Test wicket. After Zaheer had hooked and skied Lawson, Azeem fended at Lillee and Marsh, who had been rather out of things, gleefully accepted his 350th dismissal in Test cricket. Pakistan were all out for 278 and now, as the players walked off, Greg Chappell was met when he came through the gate in front of the pavilion by his brother Ian with microphone in hand. He said in front of the television cameras that at the end of the match he was going to retire from Test cricket. In effect, he went on to say that he had had enough and that it was becoming harder for him to keep up his enthusiasm for the game. When I travelled to the ground with him on one morning of the match, he told me that the prospect of having to travel all round Australia during the Benson & Hedges World Series Cup over the next six weeks had finally persuaded him to call it a day.

After Chappell's quiet and dignified exit from Test and international cricket came the news that Dennis Lillee was preparing to announce his retirement – but only to the newspaper which made the highest bid. With Lillee aware of the financial possibilities of every situation right to the end, his agent Austin Robertson must have had a busy time on the telephone. In the end the story appeared in the *Sydney Sun* for which Lillee was in any event writing. The second day's play in a Test match which had developed into a final parade of war veterans, was preceded by a press conference in the Noble Stand at which the great man talked of his retirement and the hope that he could not only spend much more time with his family but that he could also lock himself away on the farm he had bought in Western Australia. Dennis Lillee with straw in his hair was quite a thought. So, while Australia and Pakistan continued to fight out the Fifth Test, we put our heads down in order to write our eulogies or farewells to Dennis Keith Lillee who was no less a genius with the ball than Greg Chappell was with the bat, although rather a different man at the back of it all.

Kepler Wessels and Wayne Phillips had made six for Australia in the last few minutes on Monday evening and only five more had been scored when Wessels drove at Azeem Hafeez and was caught behind off the inside edge. Azeem was only twenty and was an exciting prospect as a left-arm fast bowler. He is tall for a Pakistani and as he thickens out his pace will increase. He is already able to move the ball both ways and has a knack of producing the occasional one which is good enough for anyone. His is a remarkable story for he was born with a badly deformed right hand which is almost no use to him and it says a lot for his courage that he has kept going through school and club cricket to reach the first-class game let alone Test cricket. Shortly after dismissing Wessels he had the bad luck to have Graham Yallop dropped in the gully by Sarfraz whose reflexes, or maybe his concentration, were no longer as sharp as they once had been. Australia had reached 66 when Yallop drove at Mudassar and was caught behind by Wasim Bari, another old faithful who turned out to be playing his last Test, for on returning to Pakistan at the end of the tour he too announced his retirement. He had played in 81 Test matches, which is more than any other Pakistani, and because of his modest approach had often gone unnoticed.

Yallop's departure heralded the final appearance of Greg Chappell, the batsman, in Test cricket. He was cheered all the way to the middle by a crowd of almost 18,000 on an overcast morning. Soon everyone breathed a sigh of relief when he pivoted and pulled a short one from Abdul Qadir for four. After a quiet start he was seven not out at lunch. Immediately afterwards Phillips, who is a lovely upright stroke-player with a touch of elegance which seems to be the prerogative of left handers, played back to Sarfraz and was tidily caught by Salim at second slip. Hughes joined Chappell and it was about now that I began to get the feeling that Chappell had been struck by the sense of occasion and was determined to do it justice. Almost perceptibly he changed gear. A delicious square cut off Sarfraz went away for two, he hooked Azeem most dismissively for four and with a leisurely, almost regal flourish he came forward to Abdul Qadir and although he hardly appeared to hit the ball, it raced away between the fielders to the cover boundary. It was not that it was any different from countless similar strokes Chappell had played in thirteen years of Test cricket. What made it different was that we knew as we watched that we were seeing this particular manifestation of perfection for the last time. This realization heightened the sense of enjoyment. Someone whom perhaps we had all taken for granted for too long simply because his elegance was so familiar, was now at the end holding his audience spellbound stroke by stroke, ball by ball. Rather surprisingly he reached his fifty by cutting a full toss from Abdul Qadir for a single.

The strokes continued to flow off his bat effortlessly, almost lazily, the product of supreme timing. Then, at four minutes past five, Chappell pushed Sarfraz into the covers and set off for a run which a hasty pick-up and throw by Mohsin turned into a three with the overthrows. Chappell thereby took his aggregate in Test cricket to 6,997, which was one more than Don Bradman's although Chappell was playing in his eighty-seventh Test while Bradman scored his runs in only fifty-two. Later that evening Chappell, who has never set great store by statistics, admitted that he might have passed Bradman's aggregate but that no one would ever approach Bradman's record. Earlier in this same season another of Bradman's records had been broken when India's Sunny Gavaskar scored his thirtieth Test hundred against the West Indies. He said afterwards that if Bradman had played in 98 Test matches, he would have made 75 hundreds.

At the close of play that night Chappell was 79 not out and Australia had made 242/3 with Hughes playing well at the other end but in the circumstances he was almost unnoticed. In the first over the next day Chappell square cut Azeem for four just as we were settling into our seats and then as if to remind us that he was human after all, he drove and the ball flew off the edge in the air through the slips for four more. But two balls later he put the record straight when he unfolded another perfect cover drive which will not be bettered if cricket is played for another millenium. By now the crowd was bristling with vicarious nervousness as Chappell approached his hundred while he himself remained the calmest man on the ground. There was a slight interruption when Hughes was lbw playing forward to Sarfraz. But shortly afterwards Chappell drove Sarfraz off the back foot square on the offside for two. Then, with a lovely curving arc of his bat, he square cut Azeem for three and reached 99 by pushing Sarfraz to cover for a single. The crowd of about 15,000 held its collective breath as Azeem ran in to bowl to Chappell. The ball was fractionally overpitched and Chappell's left leg came down the pitch to meet it. His bat, picked up behind him in a generous arc, came down easily, economically and precisely and stroked rather than hit the ball, decisively none the less, the product of perfect timing, past cover's right hand for four. Chappell had reached his twenty-fourth and last hundred for Australia. And on he went playing a succession of strokes which were the very essence of Greg Chappell and in so doing he reminded us for the last time of what he had given to the game of cricket. There was a brief unChappell-like moment when, on 126, he cover drove Azeem and

Javed Miandad, diving far to his right, dropped a technical chance which it is safe to say no one else in the Pakistan side would have got a hand to. A drive past cover's left hand off Abdul Qadir took him to 150 and almost incidentally Australia's lead over Pakistan was becoming significant. At the other end Allan Border played some good strokes, but went on almost unnoticed until he drove at a wide one from Mudassar and a furious appeal for a catch behind the wicket announced that he was out. Chappell's 200 seemed a certainty but it was becoming clear that he was tired and when the score had reached 436/5 he played back trying to work Mudassar to leg and was lbw. His dismissal came as a shock and a disappointment which lasted only momentarily before the crowd stood and cheered him to the echo as he disappeared into the pavilion at the Sydney Cricket Ground for the last time with a bat under his arm, leaving a matter of 182 runs against his name on the scoreboard. Chappell had joined two other Australians, W. H. Ponsford and A. R. Duff, who had both scored hundreds in their first and last Test matches.

Hughes declared soon after Chappell's dismissal, when Australia led by 176 leaving Pakistan 45 minutes batting that evening. At a quarter-past five Chappell was in his usual position at second slip as calm and as unruffled as ever. Seven minutes later Mohsin Khan came forward to drive Lawson in the second over of the innings. The ball flicked the outside edge and flew high to Chappell's right at second slip. With all the time in the world he reached up with both hands and held his 121st catch in Test cricket, eclipsing Cowdrey's record of 120. For Greg Chappell it had been the perfect day.

The last day of the match began with an announcement by Rodney Marsh that he would be unavailable for family reasons for Australia's forthcoming tour of the West Indies. Those close to Marsh will almost certainly have known that it was his intention to retire from Test and international cricket along with his two great friends and team mates, but this was his testimonial year and if he had announced his retirement now, he would not have been chosen for the one-day Benson & Hedges competition. In his testimonial year this would have cost him money. Pakistan began the last day at 47/1 still 129 runs behind and they never suggested during the day that they were likely to save the match. They could hardly have had a worse start when, before a run had been scored, Mudassar went back to one which lifted from Lawson and played the ball onto his leg stump off the inside edge. So far, the match had belonged to Chappell and to a lesser extent to Lillee, but now it was Marsh's turn to make his mark. The score was 56 when Qasim Omar pushed at Lawson and, diving far to his right as he has done so many times, Marsh held a brilliant catch in both gloves. The hundred had just arrived when Zaheer thrust forward to Hogg and there was Marsh coming up with another catch as he tumbled across in front of first slip. Imran played forward to Hogg and gave Marsh his third that morning, a straightforward chance although Imran looked less than enchanted when he was given out. Marsh's fourth catch of the day followed at 163 when Javed, after playing some good strokes, went forward to Lawson. The end was now not long in coming and with a great sense of occasion Dennis Lillee took the last four Pakistan wickets. Watching him stride in for the last time was rather like looking at an old movie. He was still a magnificent sight, and just as I had appreciated Chappell's strokeplay all the more because I knew I was seeing it for the last time, so I relished Lillee's final few overs in Test cricket. First, Salim Malik played a cut and high to his left at second slip Greg Chappell held his 122nd Test catch as easily as any of the other 121. Then, Abdul Qadir swung and Marsh stood under the skier and safely collected his fifth catch of the innings. Wasim Bari had a desperate heave and Phillips caught him at second slip and finally Sarfraz steered Lillee straight to second slip where Phillips made another neat catch. Australia had to score 35 to win and the match was over soon after tea and they had won by ten wickets.

It had been an extraordinary final Test for these three great Australian cricketers. Chappell had beaten Bradman's aggregate of runs in Test cricket, he had scored a hundred in his last Test match to put with the hundred he made in his first against England in Perth in 1970/71, and he had beaten Cowdrey's record of 120 catches in Test cricket. Dennis Lillee had taken eight wickets in the match and brought his total number of Test wickets to 355. Rodney Marsh had held six catches to bring his tally of Test dismissals also to 355, an extraordinary and appropriate coincidence. It may not have been an especially memorable game of cricket, but these three made sure that it was an occasion which will never be forgotten.

8
Three Remarkable Australians

In paying tribute to Greg Chappell, Dennis Lillee and Rodney Marsh it does not do to become bogged down in statistics which can never tell more than part of the story. It is difficult, though, to come up with anything new to say about men who became cricketing legends while they were still playing. I thought, therefore, that rather than try and rehash everything that has been said ad nauseam since they retired I would fall back on the pieces I wrote in the *Australian* on the day following the announcement of each man's imminent departure. This way maybe it is possible to keep something of the freshness which comes from writing about a significant event in its immediate aftermath. I have edited all three pieces and have made a few small additions.

GREG CHAPPELL

Wednesday 4 January

Greg Chappell's retirement from Test cricket will bring to an end an era in the game's history in more senses than one. The Chappell dynasty has ruled Australian cricket since Ian Chappell took over the captaincy from Bill Lawry for the last Test against Ray Illingworth's England side in 1970/71.

Greg succeeded Ian for the series against the West Indies in 1975/76 and heralded his appointment with a century in each innings in the First Test in Brisbane. Recently, he has become more and more pre-occupied with business and less inclined to face the rigours of touring overseas.

He and Kim Hughes have therefore played a game of musical chairs with the captaincy, but whenever Greg has been available the job has been his. Although this apparent picking and choosing may not have pleased everyone, it is the Australian Cricket Board and not Greg Chappell who has selected the captain. Greg merely told the Board that he was available.

His final joust with the captaincy was on the short tour of Sri Lanka last year and now, after what has for him been only a reasonable series against Pakistan, he has quite understandably decided that he has had enough. In a sense, the Chappell era will not end completely until Dennis Lillee and Rod Marsh also retire, but the departure of Greg to all intents and purposes signals the end of the powerful Australian side which came together in the mid-seventies.

When the news of Greg Chappell's retirement reaches all the distant corners of the Test-playing world it can only produce a feeling of sadness. Greg was one of the truly great batsmen in the history of the game – a lovely, upright, elegant strokemaker built in the true classical mould. He was a batsman too who gave a joy to those who were lucky enough to have watched him which, thank goodness, could never be measured in anything as mundane as bare statistics.

His strokeplay brought with it an aesthetic enjoyment which of all his contemporaries perhaps only South African Barry Richards and his West Indian namesake, Viv, could match. And yet perhaps Greg's strokeplay was more beautiful than either for he was simply the ultimate coaching book brought to life. Whereas the two Richards lived joyously on improvization, Greg Chappell has done no such thing for the simple reason that he has never had the need to.

Few batsmen in the game's long history have been able to play the on-drive with the perfection of Greg Chappell. It has not been the gift of many batsmen to see the ball so early and to play every stroke with so much time to spare. It is probably true to say of Greg Chappell that never in his batting life has he made an ugly movement.

His judgement, his footwork and therefore his balance have been faultless and the sum total of all his movements have been that unlikely combination – objects of great beauty and ruthless extermination.

I think that one of the principal reasons for the enjoyment of the game of cricket is the sheer beauty of classical strokeplay when all the batsman's movements are welded together into a single work of art. It would be fair to say that no art gallery in the world would ever have turned away a single stroke played by Greg Chappell.

In a sense, there is an aesthetic connection between an on-drive played by Greg Chappell and the ballet Swan Lake danced by Rudolf Nureyev. Some may say that this is being fanciful, but this is what his strokeplay has meant to me and what his retirement means in that I shall no longer have the pleasure of watching him bat.

It is fair to say that if the entire art of batsmanship was ever lost to mankind and some future generation discovered a film of an innings by Greg Chappell they would be able to deduce from it the full art of batsmanship. There have not been many batsmen about whom one could have said this.

Of course, in time, others will come along and in, say, twenty-five years, it will be written of a player who is perhaps unborn today that not even Greg Chappell could have played a better on-drive. But then, like all other aspects of life, cricket is involved in a continuing evolutionary process.

No eulogy of Greg Chappell would be complete if it was not tempered slightly with a reference to a competitive spirit which was so strong that it produced that underarm ball against New Zealand at the Melbourne Cricket Ground in 1980/81 in the finals of the Benson & Hedges competition. With the last ball of the match to be bowled New Zealand needed six runs to tie, a result which would have meant that all five of the finals would have had to have been played.

Trevor Chappell was the bowler and Greg instructed him to bowl an underarm grub at Brian McKechnie who could do nothing but block it and Australia won the match. When Chappell comes to look back over his career this is the one action he will regret. It was the only occasion when he let down a game he has so splendidly adorned.

Comparisons are invidious and always will be, but just for one moment I should like to ask time to stand still. Then, I can savour Greg Chappell, every inch a lithe, natural athlete, walking down the pavilion steps at Lord's, the Sydney Cricket Ground or wherever.

I can see him taking guard and then standing at the crease waiting for the bowler in that delightful angular way of his. Next the left leg will move forward, the bat will follow in a graceful yet authoritative arc and mid-on will trot back to the boundary to fetch the ball.

That is the Greg Chappell I shall remember and I hope that all others lucky enough to have seen him bat will treasure the memory with me. I shall also remember the nonchalant ease with which he pouched those catches in the slips before casually, almost disdainfully throwing the ball aloft. There was also that seemingly innocuous slow medium seam bowling which brought him 47 Test wickets.

In fact, Greg, thanks for the memory and over the next three days please give us just one more to take home and put in the bottom drawer. And have a happy retirement.

DENNIS LILLEE

Thursday 5 January

It is bad enough to think that we will never again see Greg Chappell's elegant strokeplay in Test cricket, but Dennis Lillee's retirement will leave at least as big a gap. Since Lillee first played for Australia against England in 1970/71, he has never been far away from the headlines. He has been a glorious fast bowler, perhaps the best of all time, with the most perfect run-up and action which has claimed 355 Test wickets.

He is also a man of extraordinary courage and determination who, early in his career, overcame a back injury which would have ended the playing days of most fast bowlers. On several other occasions since recovering from that injury, he has defied medical odds and fought back to full fitness just when it had looked as if injury must finish him.

Then, of course, there is the rather more unpalatable side of Lillee. The ardent headline-seeker who more than once has tested the patience of authority to the very limit. It was Lillee as much as anyone who developed the gentle art of 'sledging' to its present levels and he has never wasted the chance of telling a batsman what he thinks of him.

There was the time he threw that aluminium bat in Perth (strictly for advertising purposes) during a Test match against England and the occasion when he kicked the Pakistan captain, Javed Miandad, when he was batting in another Test in Perth. Dennis Lillee has always been fiercely his own man. He has never cared a jot for pomp and ceremony, for coats and ties or convention in any shape or form.

It was Lillee who stepped forward and asked the Queen for her autograph when he was introduced to her during the Centenary Test in Melbourne in 1977. Yes, whatever he has done, on the field or off, Lillee has been perhaps the most newsworthy cricketer of all time. Above all, he has been unable to abide journalists who have been what he has considered to be unjustly critical of him – as I know only too well to my cost!

The truth is, I think, that Lillee has devoted his whole life to the art of bowling fast and as far as the rest of it is concerned, he strides along looking neither to the left nor to the right and he doesn't give a damn. If Lillee had not been the man that he is, I am certain he would not have been the bowler he is either. You cannot have one without the other.

I have not seen another cricketer who has had such a compelling influence on the crowds who have watched him, especially those in Australia where spectators have identified with him in an extraordinary way. When Lillee has appealed they have appealed with him; when he has felt he has been badly treated by an umpire, the crowd has felt just as let down. Then, when he has committed some of his worst excesses the crowds have seemed to idolize him even more. They love him because he doesn't give a damn and they know it.

Lillee has always been an iconoclast who has thumbed his nose at tradition. The crowds have known this and have got a vicarious kick out of it. Everyone probably has a small part of them which wants to cock a snoop at those in charge but few dare to do it. Australian crowds have found in Lillee a hero who has done it for them and they have identified with him even more strongly because of it.

The chant of 'Lil-lee, Lil-lee, Lil-lee' will be heard no more around the Test arenas of the world when this present match is over. As Lillee departs one great big spark of cricketing life will be extinguished with him. Test cricket against Australia will be infinitely duller without him. Headline-writers will find life harder, opposing batsmen will breathe more easily and even if some of the authorities will give an audible sigh of relief that they no longer have to cope with his tantrums, they will be sad that the biggest box office drawcard in the game's history has gone.

The television audiences will be sad too, for I doubt if any other individual in the history of the game has himself turned on so many sets just as he has started the turnstiles furiously clicking over on every ground he has played.

There is so much of Lillee to remember. But I shall always treasure the memory which will for ever be etched in front of my eyes of that glorious and noble action. As Lillee starts in the crowd begins to chant and 'Lil-lee, Lil-lee, Lil-lee' rises to a crescendo as he bears down on the crease smoothly accelerating with every step.

All through his run-up he is steadily attaining an irresistible momentum and one can almost feel the rhythm and the growing surge of power just as an aeroplane moves down the runway for take-off. Finally, the left arm shoots out towards first or second slip and the right arm comes over the braced front shoulder in a movement which combines grace, beauty and power.

Then, in a kaleidoscope of movement the batsman fences in hope, Rod Marsh dives thrillingly to his right and somehow clutches the ball and the hands of the slips shoot into the air as the appeal is screamed at the umpire. As Lillee shudders to a halt in his follow through he swivels round in the same motion bending at the knees as he yells his own appeal and furiously glares at the umpire. At the same time both his hands come up above his head anticipating the umpire's decision as, with both index fingers raised, he gives the batsman out himself.

When the umpire's own arm and finger confirms Lillee's views, he is submerged by his exultant colleagues and the crowd goes mad. Ninety-five of his 355 Test wickets have been taken in just this way. For me, this sequence captures the compelling and infectious essence of Dennis Keith Lillee - an essence which, love or hate him, we will see for the last time these next few days and all of us will be unable to believe that it will be for the last time.

Just as one day another batsman will play an on-drive like Greg Chappell, so another fast bowler will eventually come along with an action like Dennis Lillee's. But somehow I doubt there will ever be another Dennis Lillee - a man who has combined genius as a bowler with a magnetic crowd appeal and his own energetic, extrovert form of larrikinism. No one could ever ignore Lillee.

The Australian public has loved him, warts and all, and as a character it will be impossible to replace him. Like Marsh, Lillee deeply espoused Kerry Packer's cause at the time of the founding of World Series Cricket and Lillee the man as well as Lillee the bowler was essential to the cause and the success of WSC. It provided a natural outlet for his determination to beat authority.

As a bowler pure and simple, he will be impossible to replace for genius of this magnitude comes along very seldom and all I can say, as I said to Greg Chappell yesterday, is thanks Dennis for the memory. There will never be another like you.

RODNEY MARSH

Monday 6 February

I wonder if Rod Marsh found the experience of playing for Australia in this year's Benson & Hedges World Series Cup without Greg Chappell and Dennis Lillee too lonely for his liking? Marsh is now the last of the three to announce his retirement. They all began their Test careers in the same season, against England in 1970/71, and now they have all decided to bow out at the end of the same season too. What a gap they will leave.

They have for a number of years now been the engine room of the Australian side. It will be a long time before they cease to be spoken about in the same breath and a tribute to any one of them must in so many ways be a tribute to all three.

Of the three, Marsh was probably more the honest toiler who has by sheer hard work and dedication left far behind the early and uncomplimentary, although maybe justified, nickname of 'Iron Gloves' and turned himself into one of the outstanding wicket-keepers in the history of the game.

Statistically, Marsh has left all his rivals far behind, just as Chappell and Lillee have in their departments, although I am not so sure that he is quite so far ahead in terms of class. Marsh has had the luck over his career to have kept to such formidable fast bowlers as Lillee, Jeff Thomson, Max Walker, Gary Gilmour, Jeff Hammond, Geoff Lawson, Len Pascoe and Rodney Hogg, not to forget Bob Massie who swung the ball around like a boomerang in the heavy atmosphere of Lord's in 1972.

A combination of late movement and sheer pace found the uncertain edges of a succession of batsmen and provided Marsh with his extraordinary tally of victims. Having said that though, Marsh may have been the greatest-ever wicket-keeper standing back where he combined a slightly surprising athleticism with an uncanny sense of anticipation. It is hard to imagine anyone better than him.

For almost fifteen years Marsh has been diving here, there and everywhere for Australia like a well-trained seal coming up with astonishing catches which originally seemed to be heading towards second slip or leg slip. While the very appearance of Lillee sent shivers down batsmen's spines all over the world in this same period, Marsh's presence out of sight behind their backs will not have helped their peace of mind.

Marsh was never a dull cricketer for a single moment of his career and, above all else, his every move was filled with a bristling determination and aggression. His gruff, moustachioed ocker exterior made him a cartoonist's delight although his warm smile and friendliness often belied this appearance.

In trying to locate Marsh's position in a wicket-keeping hall of fame, he has to stand comparison with Australians such as Don Tallon and Wally Grout and England's Godfrey Evans and Alan Knott among post-war cricketers and others in earlier periods. It could be argued that they were the better all-round keepers because much of their success came when standing close to the stumps and for some of them to seam bowlers as well.

That is not to say that Marsh would not have been similarly outstanding close to the wicket. It is simply that he did not have the chance to prove himself. He played his cricket at a time when the emphasis in Australia has been strongly on pace and not spin, although his handling of Ashley Mallett's off spin suggested that he might have been just as capable standing up.

If there has been a disappointing aspect to Marsh's cricket it is that for such an able batsman his results have been a trifle disappointing. Anyone who could bat as well as Marsh when he made that hundred against England in the Centenary Test in Melbourne in 1977 should really have made more runs than he has at the top level.

Marsh the cricketer has been a supremely efficient and highly entertaining wicket-keeper who complemented the overt hostility of Lillee and who was also fiercely patriotic and gave his country one hundred per cent all the time. Perhaps no one who has ever worn the baggy gold and green cap has typified better the fighting spirit of Australia.

Marsh the man has perhaps been something of an enigma. He was a vociferous opponent of the old regime when players were not paid nearly as well as they are today and he had the comparison of brother Graham on the golf circuit close at hand. He was in all likelihood (as we have seen in chapter 1) a moving force in the formation and breakaway of World Series Cricket.

Although the Establishment and WSC came together in 1979, many legacies remained for it had been a long and bitter struggle. Marsh, Lillee and Chappell are joined together for their championing the cause of Packerism as well as for their cricketing exploits. Whether fairly or not, they may be held to be partly responsible for the change in standards of behaviour on the field of play. At times, it was as if they and the others wanted to ensure that pop cricket acquired a pop image.

But Marsh was the man who called back Derek Randall in the Centenary Test when he had been given out caught behind by Marsh himself. He was the only one who knew the catch had not carried and said so. It was also at the MCG that Greg Chappell instructed brother Trevor to bowl that underarm ball to New Zealander Brian McKechnie. As it was bowled, Marsh's horror was all too apparent. Yet he is immovably loyal and has stuck by Lillee after some of the more unsavoury incidents. His loyalty to Lillee at the present time may even have hardened his resolve to retire. (Lillee has been in trouble with the umpires in a Shield Game.)

Marsh was known to want to become the first Australian to play in a hundred Test matches and he is only four short. It would be in character if he was to miss out on this in order to back a comrade over a point of principle.

He will be badly missed, not only because of all those stupendous catches, but also because he has provided Australia's team with a major part of its character in the years he has been playing. Like his two colleagues, Lillee and Chappell, he will leave an enormous and unfillable gap and Australia will be a much less efficient and entertaining side without him. Now that he has gone he will have more time to devote to his golf and it may not be long before he is giving his brother Graham a tussle on the last green.

My final memory of Marsh the wicket-keeper will be first of Lillee steaming in to bowl to one of the Poms with four slips and two gullies crouching alongside the belligerent keeper as the arm comes over. Then follows the tentative push of the bat and the deviation of the ball off the outside edge, followed, almost in the same movement, by a flash of green, gold and white as Marsh launches himself to his right.

The slips stand in astonishment as the ball is clasped in the outstretched right glove at the very end of the dive. The victory somersault comes next and then the ball is thrown miles into the air accompanied by an appeal which sounds more like a snarl and then comes the smile as he is submerged by his colleagues.

One more batsman heads back to the pavilion caught Marsh bowled Lillee, perhaps the most famous way of all to go, but one which to the relief of batsmen everywhere has only a match or two more of state cricket to play before it moves into a well-earned retirement. No one who saw an innings by Chappell, a spell by Lillee or a catch by Marsh will ever forget them. Now, the sad moment is about to arrive when they will all have gone after so enriching the game around the world over the last decade and a half.

9

The One-Day Yo-Yo

So, three great cricketers passed finally and forever into the record books, all of them leaving behind countless memories. The end of a Test series in Australia is not these days a time for relaxation, rather it is a moment when all of us have to try and find a second wind. Over the next five weeks the two sides who have finished the Test series are joined by a third and all three yo-yo around Australia playing one-day matches for the Benson & Hedges World Series Cup. It is the most exhausting period of the cricketing year.

By the time the Tests had ended I had just completed my two thousandth broadcast report for the season and had written a fair number of words too, but it had all been a pushover when compared with what was to come. At this point the players fold away their white trousers and shirts into the bottom of their suitcases and the coloured kit takes over. Meanwhile the media girded their loins for all the fun of the fair. There would be full houses almost everywhere we went, there would be another overwhelming display of power cricket by the West Indies, who had just paid India back for their impertinence in winning the 1983 World Cup final at Lord's the previous June, there would be any amount of short-pitched fast bowling and some questionable crowd behaviour on the Hill in Sydney and in Bay 13 in Melbourne. Although these one-day competitions almost always produce some marvellously exciting finishes, I cannot help feeling that I have seen it all before and that the excitement is stereotyped and too predictable - which may simply be a way of saying that I prefer Test cricket.

As it happened, this was not a particularly exciting competition with only two really close matches, and predictably enough the West Indies won almost everything although through no fault of their own they were made to win the finals twice. The only surprise came in Melbourne when Pakistan beat the West Indies by the huge margin of 111 runs in one of their qualifying matches. Extraordinary though it may sound, the West Indies beat Australia easily and had more of a struggle against the Pakistanis. The reason was that Abdul Qadir, confronted at last by only right-hand batsmen, bowled from over the wicket and found his best form. On the other hand Australia continued to destroy Pakistan and Qadir continued to find the left-handers a problem even though for the most part he now bowled over the wicket to them too.

The closest game in the qualifying round took place in Adelaide when, thanks to Malcolm Marshall's considerable batting ability, the West Indies managed to beat Pakistan by one wicket. The West Indies met Australia in the finals and they won the first in Sydney by nine wickets. The venue for the second, which looked as if it would be little more than a formality, changed to Melbourne. As it happened, it was an absorbing game of cricket. The West Indies batted first and made 222/5 and when the last over of the match had been bowled the scores were level with Australia 222/9. If that had not been drama enough, the events which followed were a trifle unusual. The representatives of the Australian Cricket Board eventually managed to persuade a most reluctant West Indian manager, Wes Hall, that a third final was necessary the following day. In my view there is little doubt that those in control of the Australian Cricket Board had allowed their minds to be deflected by the prospect of a mouth-watering gate of some 70,000 or 80,000 on the Sunday with takings of more than a quarter of a million dollars. Their excuse was their interpretation of the rules governing the competition to which all three sides had agreed in advance.

Initially, the West Indies thought they had won because they had lost five wickets against the nine lost by Australia, but the rules stated that in the event of the scores being level the number of wickets lost by each side would not be a consideration and that the result would be a tie. After this second match, therefore, the West Indies had won one and a half games and Australia had won half a game. The only situation in which the third match should have been played was if both sides were level at the end of the second match. But even if Australia had won the third game and had levelled with the West Indies at one and a half matches each, the rules stated that in the event of a tied series, the side which had won most matches in the qualifying round would be overall winner. In which case, the West Indies were again the winners and so there was never any need to play this final match.

It was getting on for nine o'clock that Saturday evening before a decision was reached that the third final would be played. I imagine that most of the time was spent in trying to persuade Wes Hall that it was necessary. After their tour of India and now their six weeks in Australia, all the West Indies wanted to do was to go home to get ready for the series against Australia in the Caribbean. By the same token the Australian cricketers I spoke to would have preferred not to have played this third final. The announcement when it came also said that there would now be a change of rules for the competition and that if Australia won the following day they would be allowed to tie the competition and to share the prize money. The big giveaway came when the Board announced that it was going to put up an extra 30,000 dollars in prize money for the third match. It was this last bonus which showed that they knew that this was an illegitimate contest. It was an attempt to persuade the Melbourne public that it was for real. As it happened, the public was not impressed and fewer than 20,000 turned up at the MCG, which was a form of rough justice for the Australian Cricket Board. Justice was done on the field of play too when some fine strokeplay by Gus Logie and Jeff Dujon – who, next to Richards, is I think the most exciting West Indian batsman at the present time – took the West Indies to victory. It had not been the Australian Cricket Board's finest hour.

While I was in Brisbane for the two one-day matches at the Gabba in the middle of January I was present at another game of cricket which was no less remarkable than the second final in Melbourne. On the Saturday evening I went along to the Indoor Cricket Arenas Centre at Strathpine to watch the final of the Henry Blofeld Cup which Ray Ham and I had dreamed up during the Test in Brisbane. Strathpine were playing a team from Maroochydore and this match also ended in a tie and we all had to come back again in February for the replay when a sterling performance by a local funeral director saw Strathpine home.

Another diversion from the treadmill of the one-day competition was the testimonial dinner for Rod Marsh at the Sheraton-Wentworth in Sydney. I was unable to make it but I was given a tape of the speeches which were excellent. Dennis Lillee, Greg and Ian Chappell, Clive Lloyd who got a lot off his chest about Tony Greig, Mike Coward who does a brilliant impersonation of John Arlott and has become the chief cricket writer for the *Sydney Morning Herald*, and Paul Hogan did the honours. But it was an evening which had repercussions for when Ian Chappell spoke he regretted that Marsh had never been given the chance to captain Australia. 'Hughes got the gold mine and Rod the shaft' was how he put it. Kim Hughes was in the audience and was not pleased although only too well aware that Chappell had never been his greatest supporter. Unfortunately Hughes was unable to shrug his shoulders at Chappell's remarks and from then on he refused to be interviewed by Chappell on Channel Nine out in the middle immediately after the toss which has become the modern custom. Instead he strode purposefully off the field leaving the opposing captain to chat to Chappell in front of the cameras which will hardly have worried Chappell.

One of my strongest memories from the 1983/84 season in Australia came from Perth during the two one-day games at the WACA in early February. One evening after the West Indies had played a limited-over game against a country side, eight of them came to the Garden City shopping centre at Booragoon to play the Indoor Cricket Arenas state side. A net had been put up in the big concourse in the middle of the centre which was smaller than the normal court, but was still big enough. The event had been given good publicity and it produced a phenomenal crowd. They reckoned that evening that more than 30,000 people went through the centre and a great number of them stayed to watch the cricket. I was doing the public address system with the former Surrey and England fast bowler Peter Loader, who lives in Perth. We were in position on some scaffolding at the back of the net nearly an hour and a half before the start and even then the crowd was dangerously big. It was almost impossible for anyone to fight their way through the concourse for people were packed in so tightly. Of course, some people who wanted to go through to the shops found it impossible, tempers began to fray and as they began to push it became very frightening. The West Indies plane from Northiam was late and Peter and I talked about anything we could think of in an attempt to try and keep the crowd calm. One woman was trampled underfoot and it was beginning to look very nasty when suddenly the West Indian players appeared. No one had expected such a crowd and the security and the policing were hopelessly inadequate. It was a miracle that no one was badly hurt. With their heroes present, however, the crowd quietened down and watched enthralled as the local side chalked up a notable victory. The West Indians had not played indoor cricket before but by the end they were catching up fast and I would have backed them to win a return match. In the field they found it difficult to remember that a batsman can be caught off the net and that when batting it was therefore important to keep the ball on the ground. Even so, it was astonishing to see the pace Malcolm Marshall was able to generate off a four-yard run with a ball which is a tennis ball covered with leather so that it looks exactly like a cricket ball. The agility of Viv Richards at silly mid-off was worth the journey as he pounced on the ball and in the same movement threw down the stumps at the bowler's end. The speed of his reflexes was extraordinary. Clive Lloyd, Joel Garner, Jeff Dujon and Desmond Haynes also turned out and so the locals could hardly have had better value for money.

As soon as the Australian season was over, it was time to launch *Wine, Women and Wickets*. We chose St Valentine's Day and in an upper room at the Sheraton-Wentworth Kate Fitzpatrick made a noble speech and in spite of Elton John's wedding more than a hundred people turned up. For the next ten days I sped round Australia being interviewed on countless radio and television programmes and doing my best at signing sessions which can, if no one turns up, be the most embarrassing of occasions. But it was all fun. Exhausted, I ended up in Perth for the weekend before flying on to Karachi for England's four-week tour of Pakistan where the cricket promised to be considerably less predictable and more eventful than the last nineteen weeks in Australia. I was scheduled to fly out on the Monday evening after spending twelve hours trying to give *Wine, Women and Wickets* one last shove. It was certainly hectic and I hope hefty at the same time.

10

A First Victory for Pakistan

The omens for Blotravel in Pakistan were good before leaving Australia. While I was waiting at Perth Airport for the British Airways flight, which had had a problem after leaving Auckland with the England side on board and had had to pop in for an unscheduled stop in Sydney where it spent the night while repairs were carried out, I was first given a boarding card seating me at the back of the business section. Then, with apologies, this was taken away from me and replaced with another which moved me a few rows further forward. But it was not long before that one was taken back too. Finally, after the aeroplane had landed, I was handed a magic red card which plonked me firmly into the sharp end of the aeroplane where I can only say that the champagne was exceptional.

After a quick change of aeroplanes in Bombay, we arrived at Karachi airport in the early evening where cameras flashed, garlands were hung round most visiting necks and our hands were shaken into submission. I have never seen so many people as there were in the main hall that night and goodness knows how we all found our cases and got them eventually onto the right bus. I had last seen my three disappearing though a hatch in Perth at the start of a day which already seemed to have lasted for a month. I thought at the time that I would be lucky if I ever saw them again, but one by one, as if by magic, they appeared on the carousel in Karachi.

I had met up with the England cricketers and journalists on the ground in Perth and they were all staying at the Holiday Inn in Karachi while I, thanks to the organizational genius of Leon Larkin and Luci Uriatoriu in Sydney, had been billeted at the Karachi-Sheraton. In the past visiting cricketers have viewed tours of Pakistan with some suspicion for five-star living accommodation is not always readily available. In Karachi and Lahore that is no longer true. Once I was inside the Sheraton I could have been just about anywhere in the world. I had about five restaurants to choose from, there was a delightful coffee lounge on the first floor which as far as I could see dispensed about 108 different makes of coffee, there was a charming sunken lobby where tea, coffee and soft drinks and little bits and pieces to eat were served, a quiet, secluded swimming pool and a bedroom which had five-star written all over it. On my frequent visits to the Holiday Inn, I came to the conclusion that my hotel was the first among equals.

The illusion that you could be anywhere in the world is, I am afraid, short lived and I know my Pakistani friends will not be upset when I say this. After registering at reception, the next step is to be taken to your room by a porter and after struggling to try and find the appropriate change with which to tip him, and having hung up any garment which still deserves such treatment after four and a half months on the road, the automatic pilot within me sends me scurrying off to the fridge. I opened it in eager anticipation and had a nasty shock when I found that the range on offer stretched from Coca Cola to Seven Up and on to Soda Water and back again. Feverishly, I searched through all the literature about the hotel on the writing table and a rather insignificant piece of paper told me that as long as there was fairly solid proof that I was a non-Muslim the hotel could supply me with alcohol but at a price. A quick bit of arithmetic told me that Scotch whisky clocked in at around thirty pounds a bottle. Wines and champagne were available in limited supplies on request, but the price range was omitted presumably because it was too dreadful to contemplate. The situation could hardly have been bleaker and called for some quick thinking. There and then I decided to opt out, not so much on the 'if you can't beat 'em, join 'em' principle as on medical grounds. I had knocked back gallons of wine in Australia and so I decided to make a virtue out of necessity and give my liver a well-earned rest.

My friends tried to talk me out of it, reminding me what a colossal bore I became in my occasional sorties into the world of teetotalism. But I was unshakeable and within a couple of days had become a great authority on the comparative strengths and weaknesses of jasmin tea and green tea. My resolve was severely tested at a cocktail party given by the British High Commission on our second night in Karachi. For the record, I did not weaken and lasted for 28 days without touching a drop. It is easy really when there are no bars in whose direction one

Dennis Lillee strikes a familiar pose as he claims his 351st Test wicket in the Fifth Test against Pakistan

Below The Fifth Test against Pakistan ends in victory for Australia and when it was over three unforgettable cricketers leave the Test arena for the last time with a job well done

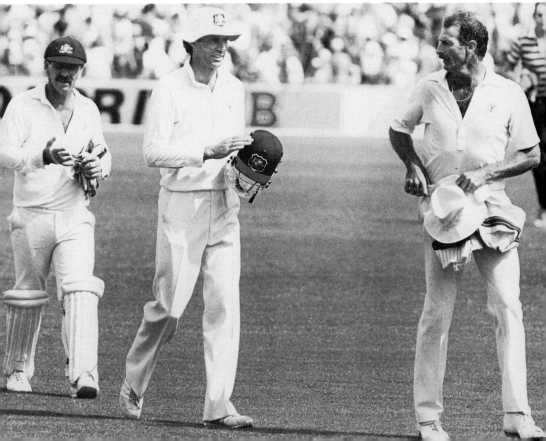

Above Jeff Thomson and Dennis Lillee, perhaps the most fearsome fast bowling combination of all, have a drink after the 1983/84 Sheffield Shield final when Western Australia beat Queensland

Below Skippers of a different sort. John Bertrand, of Australia II, believes he may have found the answer for Allan Border with his 'winged keel' cricket bat

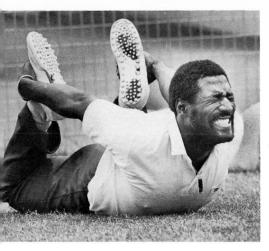

Above These days Test cricket is not only a matter of scoring runs – even for Viv Richards

Right At the end of his final Test innings in January 1985 Clive Lloyd leaves the SCG and who can blame him if he looks a trifle world weary

Below 'Not out' said umpire Ray Isherwood. The catcher, Graeme Wood, thinks Viv Richards hit the ball. Steve Rixon agrees with him, and considerable verbal battles ensued

Geoff Lawson and Allan Border were not always happy men during the 1984/85 season. Lawson's behaviour got him into trouble and Border always sprung to his defence, but with Australia winning the Fifth Test they are happy enough

A year later, after spending several months with that left leg in a plaster cast, Imran Khan was his old self as he helped take New South Wales to the 1984/85 Sheffield Shield title and the McDonald Cup

Below This extraordinary photograph was taken from a floodlight pylon while Australia were beating England in the first night game in Melbourne, February 1985, in front of 82,000 spectators. The white specks on the left are bemused seagulls

naturally seems to gravitate on returning from the cricket each evening. I was also greatly encouraged when Tony Lewis, who captained England in India and Pakistan in 1971/72 and is now a commentating colleague, also decided to take the Muslim view of alcohol for the 28 days we were in Pakistan.

I find it exciting to arrive at a strange hotel at night for I never know what I am going to see when I open the curtains in the morning. As I stood looking out over the haze of Karachi awaiting breakfast, I was surprised at how familiar it all was and for a time I relived a few incidents from England's tour of Pakistan in 1977/78. Across the road and almost directly below was the Ghymkhana Ground where, in an unimportant one-day game just before the Third Test, Mike Brearley, who was captaining England on tour for the first time, had his arm broken by a bouncer from Sikhander Bakht about whom Brian Johnston had once said during commentary that 'Sikhander's Bakht was very much worse than his Bite'. The result of Brearley's injury was that Geoffrey Boycott realized his life's ambition which was to captain England. He was in charge for the Third Test in Karachi and for the three Tests England then played in New Zealand. He found the job harder than he anticipated.

The Intercontinental Hotel also stood just across the road and it was there that the England party had stayed on the earlier tour. It had been the scene of much cloak and dagger work as the Pakistan Board of Control, inspired by the President of the country, General Zia-ul-Huq, debated what to do about the Pakistan players who had been grabbed by Kerry Packer's World Series Cricket. At a memorable press conference, the President of the Board, in a no-nonsense statement, said that his Board and the country would have nothing to do with cricketing mercenaries and that by joining WSC they had effectively outlawed themselves from Pakistan cricket. The WSC breakaway sent reverberations round all the countries which played Test cricket, but as I stood at my window that morning, I did not begin to guess at the dramas which were about to unfold towards the end of the following week in Lahore.

Later that day I sat in the sun by the pool and was joined by Tony Lewis who had just spent a holiday in India, and we sipped our lime sodas knowingly. There were a number of Europeans round the pool and one group who kept themselves very much to themselves were Russian crew and cabin staff of Aeroflot. There seemed to be several flights a day from Moscow to Karachi and back and the Russians had a considerable permanent presence at the Sheraton. It was interesting to hear the girls speak to the waiters for they all spoke fluent Urdu. When the personnel arrived in buses from Karachi airport and had changed out of their uniforms, a number of them disappeared off to the market or bazaar where they melted easily into the crowd. I could not help wondering if the same crew and cabin staff boarded the same aeroplane to take it away. It would be so easy to swop with other Russians in the crowded market who had been doing a bit of spying and were now returning for debriefing. Considering the importance of Pakistan with the Americans pouring in aid to help balance the Russian presence in Afghanistan, the Russians would be keen to find out all they could in Pakistan. Maybe an unnatural sense of suspicion has been bred in me by John Le Carré. I was in fact one of John Le Carré's most notable failures when, as David Cornwell, he had fought a losing battle in trying to teach me the rudiments of the German language while I was at Eton. He made little impact, I am afraid, with all that ghastly word order. But back to the Russians in Karachi: one evening I was told a splendid and probably mythical story about a porter in one hotel who fancied one of the Russian air hostesses. He took her bags to her room and, when the door had been shut, started upon some extra-curricular activities. The result was that he received a powerful karate chop and was dumped, like a laundry bag, in the corridor. The next day he was looking for a new job.

By my reckoning, Pakistani hospitality is second to none anywhere in the world. Perhaps they do not have five-star materials, but everything they do have is yours. Sometimes the kindness was embarrassing although the first example I had of it this time was extremely funny too. While I had been in Australia, I had forgotten to have any innoculations although I had had typhoid because of a scare in the Greek islands just before I went to Rhodes in September. I should have had cholera and hepatitis in Australia. I reckoned that the chance of cholera was remote, but hepatitis was more worrying for apart from anything else it would mean a long lay-off from booze. The Karachi-Sheraton has one marvellous institution. Her name is Yasmin Daroga and she sits at a desk in the hall and is the guest relations officer. Yasmin is marvellously homely and reassuring. She is never phased by any request or complaint and if she hears that her staff have got it wrong, she is on the telephone delivering rockets propelled by a force nine gale. Yet whatever the crisis, her smile never vanishes and however angry the guest may be, this smile and her easy manner defuses the situation in seconds. I had only spoken two sentences to her before I arrived in front of her desk on the first morning I was in Karachi and told her I needed an anti-hepatitis injection. She smiled through her glasses and told me she would let me know when the doctor would see me. I went out to the pool and within twenty minutes she came out to tell me that the doctor would see me in my room at one o'clock.

I met him in the lobby. He was fortyish, charming and with a great sense of humour. We arrived in my room and after the usual stilted conversation while he prepared the jab, I bared my arm. He said he preferred my behind and so I downed my trousers. We started talking again in mid-injection and when I was pulling up my trousers afterwards he asked me if I would like to come to a dinner party which was being given the following night by the local boss of Grindlay's Bank. I said I would love to and he promised to pick me up at the hotel at eight o'clock. He was as good as his word and his wife, wearing a colourful saree-like dress and with long flowing black hair, was with him. He drove us to a splendid house off Queen's Road overlooking the Creek. It had obviously been an important house in the days of the British Raj and, now that it belonged to the bank, it had become the chairman's house. Unfortunately there was not much of a moon that night and it was impossible to see what was obviously a superb view across the Creek which ran along the bottom of the garden. It was a big gathering, mostly of dark-suited business men with their wives, and I am sure that some of the most powerful tycoons in Pakistan were there. My host and his family were Christians and it was an evening when teetotalism was optional although I managed to confirm my new-found loyalty to Coca-Cola. I was minutely cross-examined about cricket matters especially when it was discovered that I had watched Pakistan's dismal performances in Australia.

Parties in this part of the world have a slight sting in their tail which can prove quite a trap for unsuspecting Europeans. There will be nothing mean-spirited about the measures of whisky or whatever which you are given when you arrive, and refills come thick and fast. There is a moment when the unknowing begin to hope that food will not be far away as the need for blotting paper increases. But no moves are made in that direction and while one makes a conscious effort to drink more slowly, one begins to wonder if one has misheard the invitation and that it was to drinks and not dinner. By half-past ten one is convinced that one has it wrong and the situation is becoming anxious. Then, miraculously, something is said and everyone races for the dining room where every available table is groaning under the weight of countless steaming dishes all with different and exciting delicacies. This particular evening my hostess had assured me that they did not eat very hot food in her house, which slightly disappointed me as I love it as hot as it can be. Even so, there was a succession of the most delicious blend of tastes and there was one dish of hot tongue which I thought was the pick of the night. The next surprise is that as soon as dinner is over the assembled company departs at once for home. The habit is known to foreigners in those parts as 'eat it and beat it'.

I had forgotten that this was how it happened and was beginning to wonder if we would ever get dinner when I was introduced to Shaukat Tarin who is a pretty considerable figure in the Citibank in Karachi. We talked energetically about cricket and he was one of those people who it was clear was going to become a friend after only two sentences. The dinner when it arrived was a buffet affair and we ate together while he talked me through each of the enticing dishes. As soon as we had finished he made a fast getaway and promised to drop me at the Sheraton for I did not want to be too late with the First Test starting the following morning. On the drive back Shaukat asked me to have lunch with him at one of the big hotels on the rest day of the Test match. I said that I would love to, but with great impertinence asked him if it would be possible to eat at a Pakistani restaurant and eat local rather than Western food. By the time he picked me up at one o'clock on the Monday, England had gone a long way towards losing the First Test. While Shaukat was obviously delighted that Pakistan was on the brink of its first ever Test match victory over England in Pakistan, he was most concerned at how difficult it must be for the England players after coming from New Zealand and having only two days to acclimatize. Like all the other Pakistanis I know, he was most gracious in victory and later, by the time we had finished lunch, I almost began to feel that I had it wrong and that after all it was England who were about to win.

He drove me to a small restaurant called Shezan's tucked away in a narrow street in the old part of the city. We had the usual parking problem caused as much by animals and bicycles and by the sheer weight of people as by other cars and the process was orchestrated by a constant blaring of horns. I must say that from the outside the restaurant did not look especially promising. We ignored the room on the ground floor and climbed a flight of elderly stairs to the Kurdan Room which was a restaurant without too many frills with groups of

business men sitting at some of the tables. I had told Shaukat that I
insisted that he did the admin and that there was nothing I disliked
except bread and butter pudding and porridge, neither of which applied. First, we were given glasses of fresh orange juice and then in a
clatter of Urdu, Shaukat appeared to order enough food for an army.
It was not long in arriving either and it came, two or three dishes at
a time, and continued to come for more than an hour. It was all
superb. We kicked off with Chicken Tikka which they serve on the
bone in Pakistan, grilled, spicy mutton, a yoghurt sauce and nan. I am
never quite certain when eating this food what constitutes a starter or
a main course, but I was confident from the time it took Shaukat to
order that there was plenty to follow. The temptation is always to
gorge oneself on the first few dishes and to have no room for the rest.
Sure enough, lower down the order some vegetable curry was followed
by some excellent spiced sausages with various side dishes and the tour
de force, a dish of lamb and ginger which produced a mind-boggling
combination of tastes, came last. We rounded it all off with cups of
green tea. I shall not have a much better meal at any time during the
next twelve months or a more interesting host.

We talked about cricket for a long time and then we moved on to
politics. Shaukat was most interesting about the recent political history
of Pakistan and the leading figures involved. Towards the end of lunch
I asked Shaukat if he thought there was any way I might avoid the
dubious delights of Ray's Hotel in Faisalabad where the press corps
were being housed for the Second Test. His immediate reaction suggested that there were more salubrious spots than Ray's. He went on
to say that he would suggest that I should stay at his bank's guest
house since Faisalabad, formerly Lyallpur, only boasted two hotels,
Ray's and The Ripple, and he was not especially enthusiastic about
either. He told me that the Aga Khan was building a four-star hotel in
the city and that we would be all right next time. Meanwhile busi-
nesses in Faisalabad have their own guest houses to accommodate their
own visitors. Shaukat was confident that he could arrange for Tony
Lewis, Johnny Woodcock and myself to stay in the Citibank Guest
House although I could not help wondering if it had not, along with
several others, been requisitioned by the Government on behalf of the
Pakistan Board of Control. The next day he called and told me that
this was exactly what had happened, but that all was well for he had
arranged for three of the new suites at the Ripple Hotel to be set aside
for us. It looked as though this was another huge success for Blotravel,

but, as you will see, these were only the opening shots in a hard-fought campaign.

On the evening of the rest day Tony Lewis and I went to dinner with the Radio Pakistan commentator Iftikhar Ahmed who, in real life, is chairman of Singers in the whole of South-East Asia and he spends his life commuting between Karachi and Kuala Lumpur. At dinner I met a prosperous-looking chap who Ifty described as an oil magnate when he introduced us. At Ifty's persuasion, the magnate promised to arrange a wild boar hunt for me on my return to Karachi at the end of the tour for I had been determined to have a go at the boar ever since Ifty and Imran Khan had suggested it in Australia. Majid Khan was at Ifty's that evening and he also promised to lay on a boar hunt when I was in Lahore and so the next few weeks promised plenty of incident.

I had not been in New Zealand but reports of England's defeat on a poor pitch in the Christchurch Test had been most discouraging. I gathered that it was the failure of our bowlers, and Ian Botham in particular, to make any impact on the first day which had in effect cost England the match. Now the side was starting a Test in Karachi after only two days in which to acclimatize to the change in conditions and it did not prove a happy experience on another poor pitch. England won the toss and batted and with only David Gower making any impression against the leg spin and googlies of Abdul Qadir, England were bowled out for a most disappointing 185. Qadir had bowled beautifully and now that he was back on his own native heath showed all the confidence he had so damagingly lacked in Australia. Sarfraz also bowled beautifully showing that at an admitted age of 35 he had lost none of his skills as he conjured movement out of this slow surface.

A splendid piece of left-arm spin bowling by Cook now kept England in the match although Mohsin Khan made a good half century and Pakistan lost their sixth wicket at 138. Salim Malik, who at the age of almost twenty-one looked a wonderful player, was joined by Abdul Qadir. Qadir, who is known to have little affection for fast bowling, was now allowed to swing his bat at Cook for longer than made sense and at the other end Willis persisted with Botham who bowled badly. Willis found it difficult to view Botham's bowling with a dispassionate objectivity just as he had apparently done in New Zealand's first innings at Christchurch. The result in Karachi was that Pakistan took their score to 277 and a lead of 95 which in the conditions was always likely to be enough.

Sarfraz was quick to underline England's discomfort when he removed both openers before the close of the third day. On the fourth, Gower was once again the only batsman to play Abdul Qadir with any amount of thought and reached his second fifty of the match. England were all out for 159 which left Pakistan to score a mere 65 to win. Several of the experienced batsmen in the England side made little or no attempt to try and work out a way of playing Qadir even if they were unable to read his spin. It was extremely disappointing. Pakistan then set about what seemed little more than a formality. Seventeen runs were on the board when Cook was brought on. Immediately Qasim Omar slashed at a short one and was well caught by Botham at first slip. One run later Mohsin Khan went back to pull Cook and was bowled when the ball kept low. Cook had two for nought in two overs. Pakistan had struggled to 26 when Zaheer tried to cut the ball which Cook makes go on with his arm and was comprehensively bowled. The Pakistan batting was now riddled with nerves while England busily regretted that the target had not been even 87.

They had reached 38 when Salim Malik, who was batting with some composure, drove Cook to mid off and ran. His partner, Wasim Raja, did not move out of his crease and Salim was easily run out as he tried to get back. This was a wicket brought about by the pressure of the situation. At the same score Wasim's brother, Rameez Raja, pushed forward to Vic Marks and was caught by Botham at first slip. Only two more had been scored when Wasim came down the pitch to drive Cook and succeeded only in skying the ball to Cowans at long off. Pakistan were now 40/6 with defeat a distinct possibility. But wicket-keeper Anil Dalpat and Abdul Qadir now added nineteen precious runs before Qadir made room to cut Cook and was bowled. This brought in Sarfraz and with something of a buccaneering swagger he immediately carved Cowans away past third slip for four and Pakistan had limped to their first victory against England in Pakistan by three wickets. It was a narrow squeak with their poor second innings taking some of the excitement away from Pakistan's triumph. For England, it could and should have been very different.

11
Allegations and an
Auto-Rickshaw Ride

I caught the lunchtime aeroplane to Lahore two days after the Test had ended and typically my bag was last off a DC10 which had not had a single empty seat on the flight from Karachi. I pushed it through the exit on a trolley and was greeted by a friendly shout from Farooq Mahzer, a celebrated Pakistan sporting journalist. I had not seen him since I had been in Pakistan six years before and it was a splendid surprise to find him at the airport. I was staying with Sarfraz Nawaz in Lahore and Farooq had come with him to meet me. He took me back to the car where Sarfraz was sitting behind the wheel and for a while now I became caught up in Pakistan cricket politics. We drove first of all to the headquarters of Servis Shoes, which is not far from the cricket ground, the Gadaffi Stadium, and on the upper floor we found Ijaz Butt, the secretary of the Lahore Cricket Association and until recently the chairman of the Test selectors, smoking furiously at his office desk. He was clearly harassed and a conversation which was typically Pakistani now ensued. It was carried out in Urdu and I could not understand a word, but the passion was there for all to see. Ijaz had been replaced as chairman after the Australian tour and now the consensus seemed to be that by losing seven wickets in scoring 65 for victory in the First Test, Pakistan had emerged with little credit. This was, I felt, probably nothing more than the well-known sour grapes. We were given some tea and then two guys from the sales office of the Lahore Hilton arrived.

From time to time Sarfraz explained to me what was being said and in the following argument it was clear that the Hilton Hotel was coming off second best. At the very last moment the Pakistan team had been prevented from staying at the Hilton because the Government had suddenly requisitioned their rooms for a visiting party of Chinese politicians. The cricketers had moved to the Intercontinental which had offered the Board lower rates than the Hilton. These two had come to see Ijaz to try and make sure that the Pakistan side returned to the Hilton for the Test. Much arguing, raising of voices and waving of arms - which inevitably happens in any conversation in Pakistan and is no indication of flaring tempers - ensued and even without a word of Urdu I could tell that the hoteliers were fighting a losing battle. As the afternoon progressed, more people kept popping in and had their say on a number of subjects and after Sarfraz had acquired a hefty wadge of tickets for the one-day international the following day, we departed, first for a quick look at the pitch at the Gadaffi Stadium, and then for the Intercontinental Hotel where Sarfraz had to pick up some video tapes of the edited highlights of some of the recent matches in Australia. We then drove to Sarfraz's house where I continued my relentless pursuit of Coca-Cola while we sat in his spacious bedroom watching the edited highlights of the First Test in Perth the previous November where not all the Pakistan batsmen had been as brave as they might have been. It was about a quarter to ten when suddenly Sarfraz's beautiful film star wife, Rani, appeared and we swept into dinner. Being the honoured guest, I was put at the head of the table and immediately put up a black. I was offered food before anyone else - as usual there were many dishes - and I insisted that Rani who was on my right should go first. She was reluctant and Farooq then explained that in accordance with custom I, as the honoured guest, should help myself first, so I tucked into more excellent curries.

During dinner Farooq told me the full story of all the behind-the-scenes activities in Pakistan while Imran's side was in Australia. He was able to fill in several important gaps for me and it was, as I had suspected at the time although some of the details were different, a sorry saga of interested parties doing all they could to look after themselves at the expense of the overall interests of Pakistan cricket. While we were talking, Rani got up, left and did not reappear, which was not an indication that she was bored, rather she was observing the custom that women seldom appear when their husbands have friends to dinner. Often, I would go out to dinner and leave hours later unaware that somewhere else in the house a wife and sundry children would also be eating. When Farooq, who lives in Islamabad, had driven himself to his hotel, Sarfraz went back to the Intercontinental to stay with the team and I was left with the almost impossible task of trying to tell Ashraf, Sarfraz's head of staff, that in the morning I would like tea which was weak and black. The next morning I found that I was on my own in the house and Ashraf produced an excellent breakfast although the fried eggs were rather the worse for wear following a prolonged battle in the frying pan. Before I had finished, Sarfraz's uncle, his mother's brother who is an architect, had turned up to give me a lift to the Gadaffi Stadium. Uncle Malik, very dapper, in his late forties and softly spoken, had been appointed by Sarfraz as my personal chauffeur as far as I could see. Whenever I wanted to go anywhere Uncle Malik was summoned and with great good humour he drove me all over the place. On this occasion, because I had been staying away from the England party, I had no idea of the drama which had been unfolding during the night.

At the Gadaffi Stadium, the assembled company of pressmen were looking purposeful and at once I heard that the *Daily Mirror* in London had called Peter Laker during the night about a story which had appeared in the *Daily Express* intimating that certain of the England players had been smoking pot on the New Zealand leg of the tour. I also heard that the *Mail on Sunday*, which had got wind of the same story, had sent two news reporters to New Zealand and that, having collected their 'evidence' in the form of sworn affidavits, they had arrived at the Lahore Hilton on the way home in order to confront the players and the management with what they had found. Apparently the two of them were even now lurking round the corridors and lifts like a couple of ghosts. I heard it whispered that six names had been mentioned and that the story would appear on the Sunday – it was now Friday morning. Alan Smith, the England manager, came up to the press-box on the roof of the pavilion and gave an impromptu press conference. He categorically denied all the allegations saying that he had talked to the players and he had been assured that none of them had at any time been carrying the substance. While the two from the *Mail on Sunday* continued to stalk the corridors at the Hilton far into the night, heavy discussion took place at dinner at Sarfraz's. Farooq Mahzer, Johnny Woodcock, Abdul Haye, who was the sports editor of the *Pakistan Times*, Sarfraz and myself talked it all over. Sarfraz, who was later to make the accusation publicly, suggested that some hashish had been made available to England players while they had been in Karachi for the First Test.

We heard the next day that late that evening the *Mail on Sunday* had confronted Ian Botham and Allan Lamb with the sworn affidavits which had been obtained in New Zealand and had been told in no uncertain terms to go to hell. Meanwhile the telephone lines between Lahore and Lord's had been burning as Alan Smith conferred with Donald Carr, the secretary of the Test and County Cricket Board. The Saturday, a blank day before the party drove to Faisalabad for the Second Test, was, to say the least, eventful. After two more of Ashaf's inimitable fried eggs, Farooq Mahzer arrived, told Sarfraz he was going to the Shezan coffee shop and left. Every day for years the same group of journalists and business men had gathered at the Shezan just up the road from the Hilton in the old Mall. They drank coffee and put the world to rights. Only Farooq was there when we arrived and it is fair to say that his ebullient presence together with his resonant voice will fill almost any room. Coffee and scones and tomato sauce, an unusual combination, arrived and gradually the table filled up. As a stranger my hand was cursorily shaken by each new arrival. The subsequent conversation was entirely in Urdu and it was clear that they were all great friends. Most of them were getting on in life. Before the conversation became too lively and the participants got down amidst clouds of smoke to the daily job of choosing a new president or whatever, Sarfraz took me away.

He asked me if I would like to go down to the Hilton for a cup of coffee. Eager to hear the latest news, I said I would. We went into the coffee shop and joined Tariq Saeed, the sales manager whom I had met in Ijaz Butt's office. When I popped out to the loo, I ran into Tony Lewis who was making his way to a taxi to go to Radio Pakistan and do a piece for *Sport on Four* in London. He told me there was a press conference in Alan Smith's room at twelve o'clock and said that it was important that I should be there. He knew something but would not be pressed. Sarfraz said he would wait and in the foyer I saw Bernard Thomas, the England physiotherapist, and when I asked him about the press conference he intimated that an important announcement was going to be made.

One or two other journalists were in the foyer and I heard that Alan Smith had summoned the two *Mail on Sunday* journalists to his room and told them that if they bothered his players any more he would call the police. They contented themselves, I believe, with a comment or two about his managership. Someone also said that Ian Botham might be going home because of injury. I had borrowed a Hilton biro and some paper from Tariq Saeed and we all collected in the passage

outside Alan Smith's room. While we were standing there, Botham
came out of the room next door and walked past us all grim faced
without a flicker of recognition. We then trouped into the team room
and Smith launched straight into it. 'Ian Botham is going home injured.
He has a continued degenerative condition of the left knee. Further
medical advice is essential and an operation is virtually certain.' At the
end he denied strongly to Don Mosey in front of a BBC microphone
that Botham's return was in any way connected with the recent
rumours and allegations from New Zealand.

When the conference was over, I left the Hilton with Sarfraz. First,
we dropped a video tape into his cousin's office before going on to the
Hotel International for a delicious buffet lunch. In all these places
Sarfraz was treated like some uncrowned king. After lunch we drove
to the stadium where Sarfraz had to practise with the Pakistan side.
Uncle Malik was waiting by the main entrance beside his motor
scooter and with his usual good humour he drove me back to Sarfraz's
house. After courteously saying goodbye, he drove back to the stadium, parked the car for Sarfraz when he had finished the practice, and
presumably scooted back home. He was a saint. The telephone was
ringing when I unlocked the front door of Sarfraz's house, but whoever
it was had rung off before I could get there. It might have been the
Sunday Express from London. I now wrote my various stories about
Botham's return and had just finished a piece for the *Sunday Express*
when the telephone rang again and it was Leslie Vanter, the *Sunday
Express* sports editor. He wanted to discuss the feature I had written
for that weekend criticizing Bob Willis's captaincy. He then put me
over to Colin Adamson at the news desk. The paper was naturally
anxious to get the story for themselves for the *Mail on Sunday* had
been advertising their scoop vigorously on commercial radio and television. I am afraid I was little use to him for I was dealing in rumour
and hearsay and he told me that in London they had heard about the
affidavits which the *Mail on Sunday* had collected in New Zealand
and that the two reporters were going to confront the manager and
the players who had been named in the affidavits.

By then it was three o'clock on the Saturday afternoon in Lahore
and ten on Saturday morning in London. I told Colin that I would
have my story on the telex within an hour and asked him to ring me
at half-past six my time and if there was no answer to go on trying at
half-hourly intervals. I tidied up the story adding a paragraph which
strongly denied any connection between Botham's return to England

and the pot-taking allegations. I was ready to go, first to the telex office and then to the Hilton to see if I could glean anything more, when I found I had an extraordinary problem. I was on my own in the house with Sarfraz's servants who did not speak a word of English and my own knowledge of Urdu was precisely nil. Also I did not know Uncle Malik's telephone number. It seemed to me that the only hope of getting a taxi was to ring Tariq Saeed at the Hilton and get him to send a one round to Sarfraz's house. But now I could not find a telephone directory. Then in a sudden flash of genius I realized that I had the official England tour booklet which contained the full itinerary and the names and telephone numbers of all the hotels the side used.

I found it in one of the flaps in my briefcase and returned trium-phantly to the telephone. When I got through, I asked the Hilton operator if I could speak to Tariq Saeed. There was a long pause before the receiver was lifted and a veritable torrent of Urdu poured into my ear. After a good deal of conversational toing and froing I discovered that Tariq Saeed was in a meeting and that I was talking to his assistant who, although by no means fluent in English, was good enough for us to communicate slowly. All went well on a stop-start basis and when I asked him for the third time if he could send a taxi round to Sarfraz's house and that it was a matter of considerable urgency, the problem suddenly struck me. He did not know Sarfraz's address which worried me for I realized that I did not know it either. I knew his telephone number, but with Sarfraz, Ashraf and Uncle Malik in constant attendance I had not bothered to find out where I was staying. I suggested rather nervously that he should ask Tariq where I was staying for I was sure that he would know the great bowler's address. Tariq's assistant promised to ring me back, but asked me to have one last try at finding out the address from the staff.

Considerably flustered and with the hands of my watch moving round uncomfortably fast, I burst out of the front door and found an old lady who was one of the staff sitting on the edge of the top step on the terrace with a small child on each side. She seemed startled to see me, but worse was to follow for her when she found herself engulfed in a torrent of English spoken faster than she probably thought was possible, asking her to tell me where I was. Even if she had been able to understand it, it would have been a strange request. Anyway, she rose to her feet and looked at me with an uncompromis-ing expression which came through two formidable front teeth. It was abundantly clear that, as far as she was concerned, I was in a cul-desac. Taking an immediate decision, I ran to the solid metal gates of the drive, unbolted them and ran out into the road. The staff began to shout to each other while I looked frantically for a number on the gate post. I could not see one – although I later discovered where it was – and was becoming increasingly frantic as the minutes ticked by and I saw myself doomed to remain wherever I was for hours if not for ever with my story for the next day's *Sunday Express* in my hand. Then I changed my tactics and ran into the middle of the road with arms outstretched to stop a passing motor scooter. The driver looked highly apprehensive as he clamped on the brakes and probably thought I had had too much sun. I burbled at him at great speed, but he too knew no English and so I waved him on and then confronted a startled bicyclist with much the same result except that for all I knew he might have been mute for he was so alarmed that he was unable to get a single word out in any language whatever. With panic increasing I retraced my steps through the gate watched by an ever-increasing number of Sarfraz's staff who clearly thought I had gone off my head. The younger Ashraf – Ashraf the Elder had probably driven Rani to wherever she was shooting that day – came up to me in some state of agitation, but like all the others, including the old lady with the front teeth, he was extremely anxious to help. The only time I knew I understood Ashraf the Younger was when he offered me a cup of tea or coffee for he had the jug or the pot in his hand. Now, he made a flow of proposals which did little to calm me down for I understood not a word. Then, in a flash, I remembered that Tariq's assistant was still on the telephone and shot back through the front door and into Sarfraz's bedroom. He was waiting patiently at the other end when I explained my plight somewhat breathlessly, he promised to ring me back when he had spoken to Tariq.

I then took to pacing round the drawing room. Ashraf the Younger appeared from time to time looking highly nervous and puzzled at the English sahib's extraordinary behaviour. He got lots of marks for effort, but I was unconsolable. Then the telephone rang, I shot into the bedroom and it was Tariq. No, he did not know Sarfraz's address, but he solved the problem as I knew he would. He told me to put Ashraf the Younger on the telephone – he was the only one around – and he would talk to him in Urdu. By means of an extravagant sign language I got Ashraf the Younger to the instrument and a long conversation followed during which it occurred to me that Ashraf the Younger might not himself know the address of Sarfraz's house. Anyway, I got the feeling that we had run into a snag. I never discovered what the answer was for he handed me back the receiver and after a slight pause I found myself talking once more to Tariq's number two. He told me that he had instructed Ashraf the Younger to go out and find me a taxi.

Getting on for an hour had already been lost and now Ashraf the Younger set off out of the gates like a lamplighter and up the street of which more than any other in the world I wanted to know the name. I contented myself by pacing around the house hoping that the story of my pitiful lack of organization would never penetrate the walls of the *Sunday Express* sports room in London. I was standing by the window of Sarfraz's smart drawing room when, about twenty-five minutes later, a furious buzzing noise which sounded like a nest of hornets announced the arrival of an auto-rickshaw. Ashraf the Younger came through the gates with the sort of smile which suggested that he might have won the football pools while I, who at that stage would happily have settled for a pair of roller skates, leapt out of the house with my story in one hand and my cable credit card in the other. Then, of course, there was another problem: how to tell the driver where to go. I looked most apprehensively at Ashraf the Younger and said in a firm voice, 'the GPO'. His eyes lit up at once and he told the driver at least eight times that the GPO was our destination. I was by no means sure that the driver had understood.

An auto-rickshaw is a favourite means of transport on the subcontinent. There is a small perch of a seat at the front for the driver who holds one end of the handle bars in each hand. The passenger somehow crams in behind on a barely padded seat which has hardly enough room for a single dwarf. There is a thin metal roof painted in exotic colours and patterns. Mine that day was predominantly green with some exciting flashes of silver thrown in. Immediately in front of the passenger is a horizontal bar forming part of the partition between the driver and passenger. The auto-rickshaw has an engine which is a cross between a motor scooter and a motor mower and is three times as noisy. Interior springing is an optional extra, and when my friend brought his, he considered it to be an unnecessary luxury. The last and most crucial part of the whole is the driver. Without exception in my experience auto-rickshaw drivers are some of the most competitive men on earth; they are also completely mad, with an urge for self-destruction which defies description.

On first acquaintance my driver seemed OK. He was young, marginally less villainous in appearance than most of his colleagues, but he had a small and particularly nasty-looking moustache and a red and white scarf wrapped carelessly round his head in a devil-may-care manner. I was only half inside the machine when he let in the clutch in a manner which suggested that he had already taken against me. The noise was horrendous as we bumped down the road at breakneck speed and apparently, as far as I could tell, in the wrong direction. There was nothing I could do and it was clear that if indeed it was the GPO we were heading for that this was the start of an unofficial attempt on the record from wherever we had started out. I tried to sit back and enjoy it but that was not so easy. I can barely describe the next twenty-three minutes. At the end of Sarfraz's road, which was being dug up, we turned to the right in the teeth of the oncoming traffic and he never raised his foot from the accelerator for a single second. Taxis swerved out of the way, brakes screeched, lorries which I could have touched from where I sat thundered past and we were engulfed by clouds of exhaust fumes. Bicycles loomed and vanished, pedestrians cavorted and as we swung sharply to the right I almost fell out. My driver went on as if he had not a care in the world and generally exuded a confidence which he never transmitted to his passenger who was clinging on for grim death to the bar in front of him. My man pressed on. Policemen came and went, some just stood there as if resigned to their fate, one or two jumped nimbly out of the way and blew their whistles furiously at no one in particular, bicycles and pedestrians were scattered in all directions and pedestrians provided my driver with something to aim at. As I remember it, we seemed to go under a petrol tanker. At first I thought my chap was a bully for he seemed to want to take on anything smaller than himself, but after an especially close encounter with a bus I realized that he was merely an opportunist. By the way, red traffic lights posed no problem for he simply ignored them. In any event a red traffic light in Pakistan does not prevent the traffic from turning left although it is as well if the driver looks to the right as he turns. As we went on, the whole of my life flashed in front of my eyes at least once a minute and I kept saying to myself, as the Muslims do, 'inshallah' which, in a strictly non-Muslim interpretation, means 'I keep my fingers crossed'. We were, I presumed, for I had no means of knowing, getting on for the middle of Lahore when the road became wide enough to allow five streams of traffic to go in the same direction. We had to turn left at right angles although I did not know it at the time. Only the lane on the outside right allowed us up to the lights. Since we were on the inside lane, we would have to queue. But my driver, as I say, was a born opportunist; he turned right across the back of the other four lanes and then shot up the outside right. When he reached the red lights with a policeman also standing foursquare in front of the traffic, he turned at right angles to the left and buzzed across in front of the other four lanes of traffic although the drivers in the front row of the grid were revving their engines, waiting for a change of lights and a quick getaway. It was blood-curdling. The policeman looked, reached for his whistle, and then had second thoughts. In fact, if he had moved back as much as a foot we would have given him a swift one up the backside. It was a bit like taking a short cut over Beecher's Brook. Either my man was a genius or he was helped by a miracle for he did not once establish solid contact with another body moving or stationary throughout the entire journey which felt to me as if it had lasted for a lifetime. The only casualty was my bald head for every time we went over a bump, which was about every ten yards, the top of it banged mercilessly against the tin roof. It was a recurring nightmare and then suddenly we were there outside the dark rust-red stone of the GPO. My driver gave me a big grin which I returned and asked for ten rupees which I dare say was considerably above the going rate. I was shaking a trifle as I handed him a note and was then distinctly alarmed when he looked as if he wanted to kiss me. I stepped back pretty rapidly and saw that he was waving a fifty rupee note in his hand. It would have been tempting fate to have asked him for it back and I had at least been delivered in one piece. His happiness was a joy to see. I then had to cross the wide road to the telex office, a journey fraught with danger. I was half-way across when I began to wish that I had the calm head and the steady hand of my auto-rickshaw driver to guide me.

I lodged some telexes in the most inauspicious-looking telex office, but it dispatched them as quickly and efficienctly as any office I have used in the world, and then I caught an orthodox taxi to the Hilton. What had been pure and rather terrifying farce became deadly earnest as I came across groups of journalists talking in hushed whispers in the foyer. Apparently the gist of the story had appeared in London that morning in the *Daily Express* under the name of Philippa Kennedy who had been sent out to New Zealand to dig up what she could. Also I was told that the story which would appear in the *Mail on Sunday* the next morning in London had been read to the players.

They had said that eighty per cent of it was false and were not worried. For example, I was told that Allan Lamb had been accused of having a girl in his room; it was in fact his wife. Rumour again had it that six players had been named. While this was happening the two men from the *Mail on Sunday* appeared, conferred and disappeared either out of the hotel or up in the lifts. They were preparing to leave for London that night – with great irony on the same aeroplane which would be taking Botham back to England. I went upstairs to what I thought was Tony Lewis's room only to find that it belonged to freelance photographer Graham Morris who was covering the tour for the *Mail on Sunday*, the *Daily Express* and the *Star*. He told me that as he was unable to get any photographs out of Lahore he was returning to Karachi and was going on the same plane as Botham. He also said he might be back for the Third Test in Lahore. Graham Morris was a great friend of the players and a permanent part of the team room. It later transpired that the *Sun* in London, to whom Botham is under contract, had employed Morris to stay permanently with Botham on the return journey to England to prevent journalists and photographers from other papers from getting to him. He was also told not to leave Botham's side in England.

It was all pretty heavy stuff and I returned to the foyer feeling as if I really was playing a walk-on part in a film of one of John Le Carré's books. I had tea with several other journalists and was then picked up by two men who made cricket equipment in Sialkot and who had been sent by Sarfraz. Uncle Malik had been allowed a well-earned rest. We drove to Sarfraz's house. Oh yes, his address was 143A New Muslim Town; it's one I shall never forget. In fact, I never found a taxi driver who knew straight off where it was and I had further adventure trying to get back there late one night when we were next in Lahore.

12
And So To Faisalabad

After all that, the Sunday should have been an anti-climax, but the *Mail on Sunday* had been printed and everyone in Lahore was anxious to know just what had been said. The Press Association was going to telex the entire story to Graham Otway at the Hilton. My own day began with Ashraf the Elder bringing me a jug of freshly squeezed orange juice and a thermos of strong black tea. I waited until Sarfraz and Rani had left their room, then I nipped in and rang the Hilton. There was no answer at first on Otway's telephone which soon afterwards became permanently engaged, so I called Johnny Woodcock who told me that as far as he could gather the whole thing had been rather a non-event. Apparently the *Mail on Sunday* had got many things wrong, the affidavits did not confirm a great deal, while it appeared that Ian Botham was the principal target. The headline had said that he had been involved in a drug scandal and lower down it was suggested that he had had access to cocaine. He also told me that Alan Smith was giving a press conference at eleven o'clock.

As I needed to go to the Hilton, Uncle Malik appeared, cheerfully resigned as ever to his new-found role and drove me to what had in a sense become the battlefield. I went up to Graham Otway's room and found that he had heard the accusations which had been made by the *Mail on Sunday* but so far had not received a copy of the story on the telex. He told me that at the press conference he was going to confront Alan Smith with each of the accusations. We foregathered in the team room at the appointed hour and Smith, who was looking anything but relaxed, said he was not going to start the proceedings until Norman Gifford, his assistant, was present. We waited about ten minutes, and when Gifford had taken his seat at the manager's side, Smith told us that we had a duty to listen carefully to the statement he was going to read out and he wanted Gifford as a witness to what he was going to say. Without trying to be in the least uncharitable to a manager who was doing his best to do a nearly impossible job, he made a prepared statement which sounded a trifle pompous and a little difficult to understand. I imagine he was trying to warn us about the laws of libel which, in the circumstances, was mildly impertinent. I wish that when he had finished speaking I had asked Gifford what he had understood by this statement. It had been difficult to follow.

After Smith had spoken, the meeting was thrown open and when the allegations were put to him, he and Gifford went into a long huddle and produced the following statement: 'These are serious and damaging allegations which I have not had the chance to examine thoroughly. They will be examined by the Test and County Cricket Board and obviously we will be party to that examination. Please remember I have not seen the text in full and have not had the chance to look into all the comments. With the limited information I have, I believe some of these allegations are just not true. Certain matters may well now be becoming *sub judice* and without further advice I shall say no more.' I could not help but feel that this statement admitted, therefore, that at least some of the allegations were true. In the course of the whole saga in Pakistan I could never make up my mind for sure who knew more than they were prepared to say. In any event, this was a press conference which aroused suspicions still further.

The likely problems and hardships of Faisalabad had been pushed into the background by the time we all boarded the two buses at one o'clock and, with a police escort, left the Hilton. It was a typical journey in the subcontinent. The road was adequate but no more, and was dangerously narrow in parts. Every vehicle drove at breakneck speed, horns constantly blared, each village was full of people milling around the food stalls on the roadside, and the highly colourful buses one finds in Afghanistan and Pakistan were packed with people who at times were even hanging onto the outsides. The buses seemed to go as recklessly as anything although lorries and cars also knew no inhibition. There was a considerable amount of livestock too. There were bullocks and cows and buffaloes and horses and camels, in fact every imaginable beast of burden, and all were groaning under an impossible weight. There were chickens too, who like chickens all over the world love to peck away in the teeth of the oncoming traffic. There were masses of children, running around screaming like children everywhere and often with a bottle of Coke or an ice cream in their hands. There were times too when they also came closer to death than I cared to think about. Everyone – humans, animals, birds, machines – was doing his own thing at about a hundred miles an hour and with the greatest possible noise. My nerve had been hardened to all this on the drive from London to Bombay six and a half years earlier when we had travelled in a 1921 Rolls Royce and a new 3.5-litre Rover. On that journey the five of us came close to taking a pass degree in undertaking such was the standard of driving from Yugoslavia onwards.

Our coaches ploughed on towards Faisalabad, so named because the king of Saudi Arabia gave some money to the area. The police vehicle which led our convoy turned on its wailing siren whenever a hold-up seemed likely. We drove out of Lahore past the red-light district on the right and over the river Ravi before turning left and going straight on for a hundred miles or more. We crossed several irrigation canals and passed more brick kilns than I have ever seen anywhere else as well as the occasional accident. All went well for two hours provided one could stand the noise and the dust. Then suddenly the leading bus stopped, disgorging a fair number of England cricketers onto the side of the road. It had blown a gasket and after the players and the gear had been transferred into their second bus, we set off again. It was not far short of three hours when we pulled into the industrial city of Faisalabad which has been called the Manchester of Pakistan. It is a dusty hotch-potch of a city with winding, narrow streets leading off in every direction filled by swarms of people, and from a first glance it was clear that no one had wasted much time on town planning.

But, having said that, the kindness I experienced in the city was remarkable. We knew before leaving England that Western standards did not apply in Pakistan, and indeed Alan Smith had arranged for 720 litres of drinking water to be sent out from England for the players for the Faisalabad leg of the tour. Arrangements had also been made for the cricketers' food to be cooked at the Hilton in Lahore and driven up daily to the Chenab Club where the England party was staying. It is easy to become paranoiac and imagine conditions are worse than they are. Two members of the press party decided not to shave while in Faisalabad in case they cut themselves and picked up an infection from the water. By a strange irony, those who ate only the English food sent up by the Hilton were the worst affected by tummy troubles. I am sure that the spices in the local food have a considerable disinfectant value.

Our speed slackened once we were inside the city as our drivers were confronted by all the additional hazards of city life which spill out onto the road. Carts and lorries were unloading and the people regarded the roads more as pavements than surfaces for motorized transport. There was the sheer volume of people and also the animals which find their way into all cities in this part of the world. Everyone is reluctant to get out of the way for anyone else. Eventually we crossed the railway, which has to be done on entering Faisalabad either by means of a rickety level-crossing or rather a smart flyover which was the route we now took. Then we crossed a main road with our police escort holding up the traffic, before turning right into the spacious tree-lined grounds of the Chenab Club which boasted squash and tennis courts and bowling greens. It may not have been a Hilton Hotel but the locals had done everything they could to make it comfortable for the players. While the players disembarked, the press bus went back up the drive and tackled Faisalabad on its own in the search for Ray's Hotel. We had been going for fifteen minutes when the bus pulled into the left-hand side of a busy, noisy, narrow main street in front of a two-storey white building with one sign saying Ray's Hotel and another saying 'Welcome British Press'. I began to feel rather cowardly at this point, knowing that the supposed delights of the Ripple Hotel were awaiting Tony, Johnny and myself. Ray's was going to be noisy, but when John Thicknesse of the *London Evening Standard* came back to collect something from the bus, he told us that he had stayed in worse. At any rate, no one had to share rooms.

After a while the bus and the splendid travel agent who had come up from Lahore with us set off for the Ripple Hotel which was to be found on the other side of the town. We went back over the railway line and eventually pulled into a small driveway in front of the Ripple Hotel, which was quieter than Ray's being set in gardens and it was just across the road from Radio Pakistan. At this point it all seemed pretty good. I bounded out of the bus and through the front door almost knocking over the young man who was coming round from behind the desk. He smiled and shook my hand and said how nice it was to see me, which was a promising start. But then, to my dismay, still with the grin on his face, he assured me that he did not have any rooms for Tony, Johnny or myself which was less than encouraging. He seemed to know my name quite well which suggested to me that he knew about us. He told us that nothing had been written down in the book, the hotel was full and he kept saying that the reservations had not been confirmed which suggested they had been made. It was most certainly banana skin time for Blotravel and as a result I lost no time in going into my usual state of near panic. The first move clearly was to call Shaukat Tarin in Karachi. I knew I had his card somewhere and more or less emptied my briefcase on the counter but with no luck. Then I bent down on the other side of the reception area and burrowed my way into my suitcase. Shirts and socks were flying in one direction, trousers and pants in another, and everything else somewhere in between. While this was going on, Asif Malik, the redoubtable travel agent, was telling me that it would be all right because we could get rooms at Ray's. This would have cost Blotravel all credibility, and in fact we had brought up from Lahore two English cricket supporters to whom we had bequeathed our rooms at Ray's. By the time I had just about emptied my suitcase, I found Shaukat's card. The receptionist dialled the number for me and mercifully Shaukat was in his office. As soon as he heard my voice he asked me if our rooms were all right and I told him the desperate news. He could not believe it and was most upset. I handed him over to Asif Malik and he then spoke to the receptionist before the receiver came back to me. Shaukat simply told me he had been told that the rooms had not been confirmed, which he did not believe, and promised that all would be well and rang off.

I am bound to say I was far from confident when he put the telephone down, but Asif Malik now said he would call his uncle who was something important to do with the electricity board and he would arrange for us to stay in the Electricity Board Guest House. He put through the call only to find that his uncle was at prayers. He assured us that did not matter for he would now call his father who would also be able to arrange things. It was a nasty setback when he discovered that his father was also at prayers. It seemed as if it was time for Tony and I to start praying – Johnny had decided to drive up by taxi the next morning. Asif then told me that Shaukat was going to call back. In the pause that followed the receptionist, who was in this up to his ears, told me with an incipient smile that the rooms had not been confirmed and I am afraid I told him pretty sharply that I did not consider it to be in the least bit funny and would he kindly stop laughing. I also did my best to impress them with Tony being a former England captain in Pakistan. The receptionist was either doubtful or embarrassed and attended to the telephone which rang constantly while Tony, showing true Welsh grit, sat down in the television room and went to sleep. I paced up and down in the drive outside while Asif made another call and discovered that the Electricity Board Guest House had been taken over by the Pakistan team and it all seemed about thirty-three to one against. Asif now played his trump card and revealed that he knew the Assistant Commissioner in Faisalabad who had the power to requisition hotel and presumably guest house rooms in Faisalabad. Another call located him at the Iqbal Stadium with his boss, the Commissioner. A message was sent to him and the sensational news soon came back that a magistrate who had the power to order us into a guest house was being sent round. Aware that there were still untold hazards ahead of us, I told Tony the good news, but he remained sceptical.

When the telephone next rang it was Shaukat from Karachi. He was even more effusive in his apologies, and then told me not to worry for he was arranging for us to stay at the Crescent Textile Guest House. He then gave Asif a name and a telephone number and rang off. Within minutes he had called back to say that it had been fixed and that we could stay there for the six nights we were in Faisalabad which was a great relief. The next arrival through the front door was Chisti Mujahib, the Radio Pakistan commentator who was staying at the Ripple, and he told us that the Crescent Textile Guest House was better than any hotel. He also told us that the head magistrate was a relation of his and so by now we were all extremely chirpy. When, moments later, the front door opened again it was a lesser magistrate who walked through all set to roll up his sleeves and requisition us a room or two. He, by the way, turned out to be no less a person than Asif Malik's uncle and he appeared to be delighted when we told him our problems had been solved. After that it was smiles all round although I must admit that I had to clench my teeth firmly when bidding farewell to the receptionist. By now it seemed that there was hardly a guest house in Faisalabad which would not have been forced to welcome us by a magistrate or a commissioner of some sort. After handshakes all round, we climbed back into the bus and drove to the Crescent Textile Guest House. Asif was noble well beyond the call of duty for it was past seven o'clock and he was returning to Lahore that night. He also promised to let Johnny Woodcock know about our change of plans.

We twice had to stop to ask directions before finding the guest house set in small fields alongside the Textile Mills. The secretary was waiting for us and told us there were only two rooms available although he would do his best to find a third the following day. On our first night Tony and I had a room each and we agreed to double up ourselves if a third could not be found the next day. After unpacking, I joined him in his room and we were given cups of coffee before dinner. It was while drinking them and putting the world to rights that the lights went out. It was our first experience of the daily power cut to conserve energy and it lasted for an hour. After they had come on again we had a simple but excellent dinner of curry and birriyani and rice in the communal dining room along with three other guests who were as short of English as we were of Urdu. One half of the communal room was for watching television, so when we had finished Tony and I sat outside on the verandah and drank our coffee. By a set of amazing pieces of luck we had ended up in as good a position as anyone in Faisalabad.

When England sides first came to India and, after partition, to Pakistan, the party stayed in guest houses almost everywhere outside the main cities. They were essentially simple, but the bathroom worked and the loo flushed and the water was hot and the food good and dependable. The Crescent Textile Guest House was all of these things and we found it great fun to come back to in the evenings and to be able to relax drinking tea or coffee on the verandah or in Johnny's case something a little stronger, and then to have dinner and afterwards to sit and talk of this and that. The splendid Asif Malik was as good as his word and let Johnny know about the new arrangements. Tony and I were having a breakfast of fried eggs when Wooders appeared at about half-past eight having left Lahore in a taxi at half-past six. Our next problem was to find ourselves transport to the Iqbal Stadium for the Test which began that morning. The secretary who had greeted us the night before when we arrived now arranged for his son to drive us in each morning and to meet us half an hour after the close and drive us back.

Seventy years ago Faisalabad was a small village. Then the Governor of Punjab ordered a canal to be dug through it and it became a settled city drawing people to it from a wide area. It was named Lyallpur after the Governor. The city revolves around a domestic and private cotton industry which was centred on the Crescent Textile Mills. At all hours of the day horses, bullocks, cows, buffaloes, camels and sometimes tractors and lorries could be seen pulling trucks loaded with bales of cotton to the mills. Faisalabad has become a regular Test centre in Pakistan and the Iqbal Stadium is a handsome ground and will be ideal when the crowd capacity is doubled to around 25,000 –

this will happen soon. Unfortunately, the citizens of Faisalabad now had every reason to feel cheated by a pitch made of dried mud which had been rolled and rolled and rolled into submission. It was much too heavily in favour of the batsmen and boring, high-scoring draws are increasingly inevitable.

The last time England had played in Faisalabad had been on Mike Brearley's tour in 1977/78. In an uneventful match against a zonal side, Geoff Boycott had made a laborious hundred in front of about 5,000 spectators. A few weeks later the Iqbal Stadium was used as the venue for a number of public floggings which were gruesomely chronicled by John Edwardes in the London *Daily Mail*. A metal contraption was fixed up in the middle of the pitch and those to be flogged were tied to it. The flogging was carried out by a convicted murderer, who for some reason had escaped the death sentence, in front of a full house and it was said afterwards that the crowd saw more strokes in an hour than Boycott had produced in seven hours. When we were in Pakistan this time, public flogging seemed to have lost some of its appeal, for while in Karachi I had read in the paper that only 4,000 had turned up to watch a flogging in Bahawalpur.

The pot-smoking allegations, although at the front of most people's minds, were played down while the cricket was in Faisalabad. But the evening we arrived there Philippa Kennedy of the *Daily Express* flew in on her way home from New Zealand where her editor, Larry Lamb, had sent her to try and run the recent rumours to ground. She had found enough to write that piece in the previous Saturday's paper which had implied that some of England's cricketers had been living life to the full while they had been in New Zealand. She had arrived in Faisalabad to see if she could uncover anything else. When she reached Ray's Hotel, having lost all her luggage in transit from New Zealand, Peter Smith of the *Daily Mail*, who is chairman of the Cricket Writers' Club and leader of the press party on tour, insisted she went with the media to the Chenab Club for dinner, the food having made the journey from Lahore. Peter explained to Alan Smith who she was and that as she was 'one of us' he had brought her along. The England manager was flustered and called Peter Smith insensitive. Philippa Kennedy stayed for a couple of days but could not discover anything more and so returned to London. On the first day of the Test the press contingent was joined by Dominic Allen from *Independent Radio News* who had taken a week's holiday to cover this match. He had brought with him all the relevant Sunday papers from London including the *Mail on Sunday* which I gather proved compulsive reading for those who were lucky enough to see it.

England had lost the first of the one-day internationals by six wickets in front of a huge crowd in Lahore, but that was a match which was almost incidental to what was going on off the field. By the time the two sides collected at the Iqbal Stadium in Faisalabad for the Second Test, Ian Botham had returned home, and Bob Willis and Norman Cowans were respectively ill and injured. This meant that Gower, as the official vice-captain, assumed the England leadership. With only twelve men fit to play – and even Graham Dilley was doubtful until the morning of the match because of the tummy trouble which had affected the party – the choice of team was all too simple, especially as poor Chris Tavare was having one of those patches which give batsmen nightmares.

When Zaheer won the toss and Pakistan batted on the deadest of pitches, England's task was enormous. It was now that Gower came into his own as a captain. I had been told that his performance as vice-captain in New Zealand had been most disappointing and there was even a rumour that Alan Smith had said as much in a letter he had written to Lord's. It is easy to be wise after it has all happened, but there cannot have been many captains to whom it would be more difficult to be a vice-captain than Bob Willis. For a start he is, on the field at any rate, a great non-communicator. In the effort to psyche himself up for his own bowling he appears to be oblivious to all that is going on around him. If players came up and offered advice in the field they were mostly ignored. He appeared to have a close relationship with Ian Botham, who had revealed himself as no great tactical genius when he was captain of England, and sometimes he consulted Bob Taylor. Gower seemed to take the view that there was little he could do to help or advise Willis and was prepared to bide his time. He had been appointed captain of Leicestershire for 1984 and was probably intending to show his worth as a captain then.

But now, unexpectedly, he found himself in charge and on this first day the improvement in terms of leadership was marked. With Mike Gatting always eager and sometimes almost too eager to help, Pakistan were never allowed to take control and once again England had a captain who could be seen to be actively scheming for wickets to fall. Gower brought about the downfall of Mudassar when in Cook's second over he brought himself into silly point with Gatting already in at forward short leg. The pitch was not turning but Cook had

panicked the Pakistanis in Karachi and now Gower was increasing the
pressure – in the same over Mudassar gave Gatting a catch off bat and
pad for the simple reason that he allowed the pressure to unnerve him.
On the first day Pakistan were at one point 70/3 on just about the
easiest batting pitch in the world. Before the end of the day England
saw the advantage of having the odd occasional bowler in the side
when Gatting had Zaheer lbw just when he was beginning to bat
ominously well. Pakistan were 257/4 but at no stage on this opening
day had the batsmen been allowed to take control. They went on the
next day to reach 449/8 declared with Wasim Raja scoring a good
hundred and Abdul Qadir an impudent fifty. Once again the runs had
to be fought for and much time was used up. Dilley, who was still
feeling unwell, and Foster bowled splendidly while Cook did a good
containing job. At the end of the second day England were 26/0 and
well on the way to the draw which was the best result for them once
Pakistan had won the toss. The next day Gatting and Smith batted
well, adding 127 for the first wicket, although it did not prove to be
for either batsman the breakthrough one hoped it might be. Lamb's
wretched form continued, but Randall and Gower were batting well
at the close when England were 233/3 with the match nearly safe.

They proceeded quietly the next day with Randall, Fowler and
Marks playing good supporting innings while Gower was 113 not out
at the close. The Pakistanis all thought they had him caught off bat
and pad early on in his innings and generally felt that the umpiring
had been too much in favour of the visitors – it is usually only sides
which are feeling frustrated who complain. Gower was eventually out,
stumped off Mudassar, for 152 on the fifth morning after batting in all
for 427 minutes in an innings which gave the lie to those, for a while
at any rate, who predicted that the responsibilities of the captaincy
would affect his own batting. Marks made a splendid 83 and it was
sad that such a cheerful cricketer did not go on to score what would
have been a most deserved hundred. Gower's declaration came at
lunch when England had scored 546/8 and were 97 ahead. Afterwards
Dilley and Foster rocked Pakistan when they took the first three wickets for 56, but Salim and Zaheer saw pass whatever slight danger there
was for Pakistan and they were 137/4 at the end of a match which had
started most inauspiciously for England and yet by the end had given
them great reason for hope. Gower had shown that no time should
be wasted in appointing him as England's official captain, and even
though these words are written just after England have been annihi-

lated 5-0 by the West Indies in England in 1984 with Gower hardly scoring a run, I still believe he is the man to do the job and I only hope he receives the support from his players that he has every right to expect.

The only other significant event which happened while we were in Faisalabad took place in the clinic at Edgbaston in which Ian Botham had had a successful exploratory operation on his left knee. While languishing in bed soon after the operation he had been visited by Patrick Murphy of the BBC who is based in Birmingham and is a most prolific writer of cricket books. Pat had taken a tape recorder along and had asked Botham about the allegations which had been made against him and which he had vigorously denied, saying that he was too frightened even to use a pain-killing injection let alone to take drugs. He was then asked about Pakistan and spoke forcibly to the point of saying that it was the worst country in which he had ever played cricket and that he would never go there again. He spoke disparagingly about the food and the hotels and said that it was a place which it should be compulsory for all mothers-in-law to visit with all expenses paid.

We listened to this at the commentary point during the lunch interval one day and, to say the least, it seemed a little stiff. Botham had visited only the Holiday Inn in Karachi and, briefly, the Hilton in Lahore, both of which are five-star hotels. After the kindness shown to the England cricketers these comments will understandably have seemed intolerable to their hosts. Then, of course, the thousands of expatriate Pakistanis living in England will hardly have been cheered up by Botham's remarks. In the end the Test and County Cricket Board fined him £1,000 for making them and he was lucky to get off so lightly. As the Second Test ended, the wires from London were hot as Botham's words winged their way to Pakistan. One of those who was soon to read them was that fierce Pakistan patriot Sarfraz Nawaz. Another snippet of news later that same day was that Botham was intending to sue the *Mail on Sunday*, which ensured that the whole matter of the drug allegations would be an on-going story for some considerable time to come.

For me, the week in Faisalabad was the most memorable I spent in Pakistan. In many ways the Crescent Textile Guest House was more fun than a five-star, luxury hotel where one is so often just a number. In Faisalabad the three of us were looked after most handsomely by a staff of four who were all charming and they could not have taken more trouble. The food was delicious, the service excellent, the laundry was faultless and the beds were comfortable. I am sure there are people who will think I am mad when I say that I enjoy this type of simple living just as much as the five-star razzamatazz. I am not saying I want to stay for ever in the Guest House at Faisalabad, but I shall remember with greater enjoyment the six nights I spent there than most equivalent periods spent in luxury hotels.

By the time we left the three main bearers had acquired nicknames. There was Tea Cosy who was the head man and who always wore something small and ornate on top of his head. Nice Smile had a perfect set of front teeth and was always delighted to see one, while Grisled Moustache did not give away a great deal although he was especially adept at anticipating our needs at the dining room table. The morning we left, we gave presents to the three of them and also to the fourth member of the staff, who was the sweeper, and they were all so overjoyed that it was touching to see. They shook our hands again and again. Then too there was the untiring kindness of another Radio Pakistan commentator, Muhammad Idris, who lives in Faisalabad. One evening he had a party for fifty people, all of whom were connected with the media, at his charming house and we had the most delicious Pakistani dinner. At the times when we were stranded without a car, Idris either came himself or sent his son. There was another occasion when we did not know how we were going to get to a press conference at the Chenab Club and I put a call through to Muhammad Anwar, the chairman of the Textile Mills and he at once lent us his car and driver. Akram Chaudrey at Radio Pakistan did the same when I had to go to a studio on the rest day. Nothing was ever too much trouble and their hospitality put much of ours to shame back at home.

Then there was our final evening in Faisalabad when we were invited to the Press Club where there was quite a gathering on our behalf. First, we sat in rows of chairs on the lawns and listened to impassioned speeches. The first, by the secretary of the club, warned us in passionate tones against the evils of imperialism, wealth and sex. The Mayor of Faisalabad put in a strong plea in Urdu that in the future pitches should be more sporting. After that we had another excellent buffet dinner which was in turn followed by a musical entertainment. For more than an hour we listened to the sitar which was followed by a remarkable virtuoso performance on the tabla, drums played by hand. There was then a demonstration of how to play the seranghi, a one-stringed instrument with a bow. It was extraordinary that such a range and variety of harmonious sounds could come from such slender raw materials. We were all given a small seranghi to take away but unfortunately the string on mine broke the next day. The finale was a moving Punjabi love song sung by a girl. Much of the music was strangely haunting, and it is marvellous to think that those who had organized the evening, and I am sure Idris was largely responsible, were prepared to go to these lengths to look after us and to see that we enjoyed ourselves. I shall always have a soft spot for Faisalabad.

13
Sarfraz versus Botham

Transport in the East is a constant source of bewilderment, amusement and despair to Western eyes. Johnny, Tony and I ordered a 'medium-sized' taxi for the journey back to Lahore. It was on the small side of medium, of indeterminate age and Japanese make. The youngish driver had no English and, we hoped, a rather better bump of locality. The start was impressive for we left the Iqbal Stadium with a show of authority which plunged us almost immediately into the narrow, dark streets of the old part of the city. The scenes were straight out of Kipling and the atmosphere screeched with motor horns and dust in about equal measure. The little shops, built four-square into the fronts of the houses like little oblong boxes, opened straight onto streets which were hardly wide enough for more than one car and yet at the same time full of pedestrians. Some, mostly the children, were scurrying along cutting patterns like demented ice-skaters as they shot out in front of bicycles and scooters and anything else which was moving. Then there were the women who walked with a stately elegance given them by their long flowing clothes and also by their upright bearing which enabled them to carry enormous loads on their heads with complete safety. The men as often as not stood still in the front of their shops, usually smoking and always managing to look resignedly philosophical. There was the occasional beggar who, although frail and spindly and desperate for anything he could get, maintained a remarkable innate dignity. Their peace was all the time shattered by the tearaways in their cars or on their scooters who in their respect for nothing are probably no different from other such drivers the world over.

All the time, dust clogged the lungs and animals scavenged around

Australia's Prime Minister, Bob Hawke, visits the Australian dressing room during the Fifth Test against the West Indies in Sydney

Allan Border meets the press after the West Indies have won the Benson & Hedges World Series Cup. Permanent team manager, Mr Bob Merriman, keeps a careful check on all that is said

Below Australia's selectors for 1984/85. From the left, Rick McCosker, Laurie Sawle, the chairman, and Greg Chappell. Chappell and McCosker both retired as players at the end of 1983/84

The man of the 1985 World Championship of Cricket, India's opening batsman and left arm spinner, Ravi Shastri, who plays a classic cover drive in the semi-final against New Zealand

Zaheer Abbas, who has been so involved in the political problems surrounding Pakistan, bats against England in Lahore in March 1984, watched over by Bob Taylor

Below Touring Pakistan is not always the hard work it is said to be. England players relaxing at their hotel at Karachi

Graeme Fowler listens to the beat and catches up with some correspondence in the Lahore dressing room

Manager Alan Smith in the centre with his assistant Norman Gifford in the white hat watch the Third Test in Lahore while Neil Foster writes home

Left Bob Taylor and supporters during the Lahore Test

Above Bob Willis, who captained England for the last time in the First Test in Karachi, in contemplative mood....

....and in action

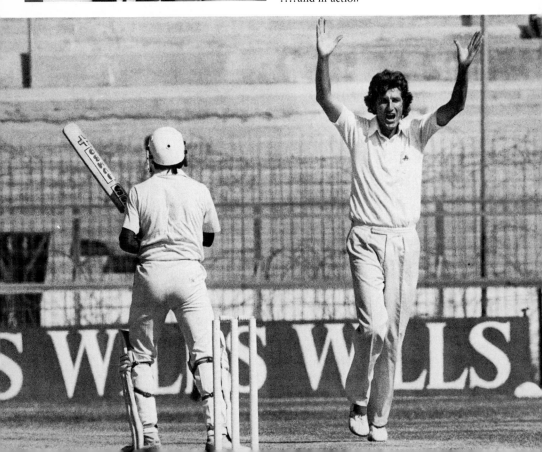

below the shops at the side of the narrow streets. Each street we turned into seemed at first glimpse to be irrevocably blocked, but miraculously our driver hooted, cajoled or swore his way through. Whether the obstacles were human, animal or mechanical they were all equally mulish. Only one incident on our return journey to Lahore needs recounting at length. All the others were, except for minor differences, as hysterical and as frustrating or as dangerous and as laughable as all incidents on every other journey of any length in this part of the world. The exception came soon after the start. After wending our way through this succession of tiny streets, we suddenly emerged as if at the end of a tunnel into bright sunlight with a small piece of open land on our right which looked as if it might have been swampy. The surface of the road had deteriorated to a marked degree. After going straight on for another fifty yards we had to turn right in order to cross the railway over the rickety level-crossing. We had come the back way in order to avoid the bridge and flyover – it was the way Johnny had come into Faisalabad by taxi. We had arrived a few minutes after the iron gates had been shut in expectation of a train and a healthy chaos was developing on both sides of the line. It looked as if one of the carts loaded with sugar cane had missed the crossing and lost most of its load for there were piles of cane on the rails which were being cleared by men who were forking the cane into the space between the rails. The wheels of the cart had apparently fallen off the crossing, causing it to lurch sideways and lose its load.

On our side of the crossing two cars had pulled up as if in a poor attempt to form an arrowhead. We nosed our way between them. The crossing itself was narrow, allowing no more than two small cars at the most. The front row on the far side had already been taken up by two huge old carts which were brim full of sugar cane and were defying anything else to pass. There were two or three men driving the carts which were pulled by buffaloes. With the gates still shut there was no immediate competition for the crossing, but the meanest intelligence could see that this was going to take some working out when the gates opened. There was more noise on our side as the queue was joined by more cars and scooters and there were a good many pedestrians standing around rather vacantly chewing sticks of sugar cane. More loaded cane carts joined the queue on the other side and then a new arrival at the back of the queue on our side began to blow his horn and this soon caught on. The sugar cane chewer nearest to my side of the car found the resulting noise extremely funny and came close to choking on his sugar cane. The original horn may have been blown by a driver who was wondering what the hold up was for, but most of those who were now joining in were doing it for the sheer hell of it. Our driver was wearing a pale green kurti camise, the traditional baggy trousers with a long shirt-like coat with the tails coming down to the knees and made of cotton. He walked over to the closed gates and peered anxiously down the line. Johnny Woodcock, a tiger for photography in these conditions, joined him on the crossing and while speaking in resonant English to anyone and everyone clicked away at the locals who loved the attention.

Johnny also began to peer down the line as if the Faisalabad express was going to whistle past at any moment, but after fifteen minutes of peering there was no sign of it. Tony Lewis and I stayed in the back of the taxi keeping a general eye on things. By now the traffic on our side of the gates was in complete chaos and it stretched back for 200 or 300 yards. It would have been impossible to have squeezed even another push bike in for it was packed so tightly together. It was impossible to see what was piling up behind the loads of sugar cane on the other side but the blowing of horns and general noise suggested plenty of activity. By now all the advantage we had gained by leaving immediately after the close of play had gone and it began to look as if we would be lucky to reach Lahore by midnight.

Then we were suddenly joined by another noise and everyone who could see was staring down the line towards Lahore. Sure enough, in a minute or two an elderly train clanked past making the sort of noise which suggested it must have had bad indigestion. It was full to the brim with people almost falling out of the open windows. The train was moving quite slowly and the noise its arrival created on both sides of the crossing made the cacophony of the last forty minutes sound like a distant rumble. As engines were started, the hooting and ringing of bells was redoubled and you have never heard such a noise in your life. At the same time a none-too-friendly jockeying for position began. But there was now another problem for the chap who operated the gate could not be found for at least five minutes. All vehicles seemed to be waiting on full throttle. Eventually he appeared and was not in the least concerned as he stood there fiddling with the wire which held the two gates together and carrying on a conversation with a friend over his shoulder. At last the rusty bolt was pulled away and then he wandered across the line and repeated the process on the other side. When the other gate was opened it signalled the start of the Faisalabad

Grand Prix with the two halves of the field going in opposite directions. It seemed quite hopeless and we were right in the thick of it,
but our driver was more than up to it. Suddenly, as if a magician had
waved a wand, we found ourselves on the crossing and as far as I
could make out without establishing contact with any solid objects
either human or mechanical. We jolted down on the other side and
lumbered on, turning right and then left onto the main Lahore road.
I cannot believe anyone else was as lucky as we were, but I suppose
that what we had just seen happens several times a day and that for
the locals it was all rather boring. I wish I could have seen what
happened to the carts of cane and how many lost their loads.

From then on the medium-sized car drove at a nicely medium speed,
which was unusual, on to Lahore. The driver kept his thumb more or
less permanently on the horn and in spite of his conservative speed he
still contrived to make it all most exciting. His pet trick was to wait
until he could see a car coming in the opposite direction before making
the decision to overtake. He obviously liked to feel a sense of challenge.
Several times we drove bullock carts into the rough ground at the side
of the road and at other times there cannot have been much more than
an inch of daylight between the two cars, but once again we never hit
anything. As we neared Lahore, a most impressive storm was doing
its stuff ahead of us and soon we were belting through water which
must have been almost up to the axle although by some fluke we never
stalled. By now cars were using their headlights which made overtaking
if anything even more exciting.

The only serious hitch came when we had turned right into Lahore
and crossed the bridge over the river Ravi. The three of us were talking
and not paying much attention now that we were almost there when
I looked up and after a moment of surprise realized that the traffic
coming towards us looked even more menacing than usual. Suddenly
it occurred to me that our splendid driver had been driving for a good
minute or two the wrong way up a dual carriageway. At about the
same moment a local policeman made the same discovery and stopped
the car. He said something pretty sharp to the driver in Urdu with the
result that we began to reverse in the dark with cars streaming past
us on the offside. By the greatest piece of luck we found an opening in
the central barrier and with profound relief we got into the right
carriageway, but only to find that our policeman was standing in front
of the bonnet with his hand up. Our driver was relaxed enough
though, and after his licence had been checked the policeman seemed

content and waved us on. Our driver knew downtown Faisalabad rather better than downtown Lahore and was reluctant to take advice, so it was a little time before we found ourselves outside the Hilton. The first new face we encountered there was that of Alan Herd, Ian Botham's solicitor, and then, after a quick snack in the coffee shop, Ashraf the Elder appeared and drove me back to 143A New Muslim Town, an address which is now permanently imprinted on my mind.

Events began reasonably early the next morning with Sarfraz show-ing me the cutting of the statement he had made to the *Pakistan Times* deploring the terms under which the Pakistan team was going to Shar-jah to play in the Asian Cup. He also showed me the letter he had received from the secretary of the BCCP asking him for an explanation since he was not allowed to say these sorts of things to the Press. Sarfraz was delighted by the reaction. During the morning we drove to Sallous, a restaurant just up from the Hilton where we drank some coffee and ate a chicken shashlick with a few of Sarfraz's friends, two of whom had played in one Test match for Pakistan some years before. Later, we were joined by leg-spinner Abdul Qadir who was as indom-itably cheerful as ever although he too had a grudge about Sharjah where he had apparently been paid less than anyone else the year before. After that we made a quick sortie to the Intercontinental Hotel where Sarfraz had a room with the other Pakistan players. We were joined there by journalists Farooq Mahzer, Omar Kureishi and a friend of his. Farooq was furious that Mudassar Nazar had been left out of the Pakistan side for the Third Test and that as a result they were going into the match with only three and a half bowlers, one of whom was so new and inexperienced as hardly to count. Sharjah came up for more discussion and there was a feeling of concern that India and Pakistan should offer jointly to host the World Cup, yet could not put on the Asian Cup. Apparently a Sri Lankan official had even said that as the Asian Cup was purely a financial gimmick why didn't the sides go to South Africa where there was even more money – he was not being serious, but merely a trifle sceptical about Sharjah's attempts to buy its way into big cricket.

Then it was on to Servis Shoes and Ijaz Butt's office where we were joined by the Pakistan Test selector Shafqat Rana. Once again Sharjah was on the agenda. We drove from there to the Gadaffi Stadium and saw where water had leaked under the covers during the storm the previous night. Sarfraz was adamant that the side winning the toss should put the other in. Shafqat came and looked at the pitch with us and talked about the time in 1961 when he had been hit by a bouncer from the West Indian Charlie Griffith which he was sure he had thrown. He had made 52 at the time and had to be carried off.

We now drove down to Uncle Malik's and were warmly welcomed as always by Malik who invited us in for tea. We sat upstairs and first we were given a piece of carrot pie which was excellent although rather filling. Uncle Malik now spoke about the derogatory remarks which had been made by Ian Botham from his hospital in Birmingham about conditions in Pakistan. Although most of the conversation earlier in the day had been carried on in Urdu, I do not think Botham's remarks had been spoken about. They had been quoted in full in an Urdu paper and had been downright insulting. At once Sarfraz was beside himself with anger and said straightaway that he would make a statement to the Press saying that Botham had been given hashish while in Karachi. Sarfraz told us he knew who had given it to him and I have never seen anyone so determined to get his revenge. Botham's criticisms of Pakistan were rather surprising in that he had stayed in two five-star hotels. Still, maybe post-operative gloom had set in while lying in bed after that exploratory knee operation.

We returned to 143A New Muslim Town to find three friends of Sarfraz's on the doorstep. They were the brothers Shah who between them owned two highly successful restaurants in Bradford. I settled down to some work while they nattered away in the drawing room and in time Farooq came booming in. When I returned, Sarfraz said in a voice which brooked no argument that he was going to make a statement to the *Pakistan Times* saying that Botham had been given some hashish in Karachi. Sarfraz said that he knew who the supplier was and went on to talk about a party which had taken place outside Karachi at the time of the First Test. He was raging about Botham's remarks and was determined to make a fiercely patriotic statement. Sarfraz was insistent he wanted no money for what he was going to say and was not therefore trying to sell the story. He wanted to make sure that what he said would make a big impact in Pakistan. He had already arranged for Abdul Haye, the delightful sports editor of the *Pakistan Times*, to come round later that evening. He duly arrived and sat on the sofa beside Sarfraz taking down some stuff which was both explosive and fanciful.

Farooq, in an armchair to Sarfraz's right, did his best to try and persuade him not to make a statement, but said that if he insisted on going ahead, he should do it in such a way as to gain the maximum effect from it. He suggested delaying it for a day so that he, Farooq, could have a quiet word with the new president of the BCCP saying that Sarfraz was determined to go ahead and to suggest that the Board therefore made a similar statement themselves. Sarfraz would have none of this. He probably wanted to appear on the first day of the Third Test, which was to be played on his home ground, as the hero who had fought for the honour of his country. While all this was going on I announced firmly my intention to maintain a complete silence for it would have been highly unethical for me to have done anything else. In time people might have said that I had used the situation to gain revenge for the time Botham had a go at me at Bermuda airport on the way back from the West Indies. Meanwhile Abdul Haye, who had a marvellous story on his hands, argued against Farooq and it was clear that Sarfraz was determined to go ahead whatever happened. Of course, as a journalist I was a most interested spectator and when Abdul Haye left with the statement written down in his notebook, he promised to return in a short time and to give me a copy of what was being used for the next day's paper. It was a statement which showed that Sarfraz was extremely angry, but he had gone over the top and had made some absurd allegations.

Sarfraz himself had over the years acquired a considerable reputation for being a problem child, and such a statement, although an immediate embarrassment for Botham and his legal advisers, was unlikely substantially to harm his cause.

While all this toing and froing went on, we had another excellent dinner which had been ferried round by Ashraf the Elder by car from Sarfraz's mother-in-law's house, and it was getting on for twelve when everyone began to depart. Farooq drove off in his car and I went with Sarfraz, driven by Ashraf the Elder, to the Intercontinental where Sarfraz was staying with the Pakistan team. I obviously had to ring the BBC and notify them of these developments and as luck would have it Sarfraz's own telephone was out of order. When we arrived at the Intercontinental, Sarfraz gave careful instructions to the taxi desk as to the whereabouts of 143A New Muslim Town, so that when I had to return my means of retreat was organized. The chap in charge seemed to understand and repeated the instructions in Urdu to Sarfraz and all seemed well. Sarfraz went up to his room while I arranged for the hotel switchboard operator to put the call through to London. There was an added complication for something was wrong with the Lahore exchange and it had to be routed through Karachi which meant

that there would be at least an hour's delay. I sat in the entrance hall
scribbling some notes down so that I would be able to do a voice piece
when the time came. I had a great piece of luck when the call came
through in only twenty minutes. I spoke to the news room and after
an interminable delay, which can often happen on these occasions – I
was terrified I would be cut off – I was put through to Foreign Traffic
and recorded a piece. A charming lady who was the foreign news
editor and had been listening to the piece now told me that it was
almost certainly unusable because of the libel situation and she said
she would give it to the lawyers. Anyway, they had the facts and I
hoped that even if they could not use it they could get some copy from
it, but the lawyers would not allow them to touch it. It is always
irritating when you have bust a gut to get a story across only to be
told that it is unusable, but it was nothing compared with the frustra-
tion I was shortly to experience.

Before leaving the Intercontinental I called Graham Otway, who
was in charge of events for the Press Assocation, and told him what
had happened. Of course he was sound asleep and it took him a
moment or two to come round. Then he said, being quite reasonably
a little wary of the story and its libellous nature, that he would wait
and read it in the morning before doing anything. When I rang off, he
had second thoughts and talked to Peter Smith of the *Daily Mail* and
Pat Gibson of the *Daily Express* and they waited up to get a copy of
the *Pakistan Times* as it came off the presses. They then got in contact
with their offices in London.

By the time I had finished talking to Graham I was exhausted and
the taxi boss whistled up the bloke he had detailed to drive me home.
As far as I could tell he went through the instructions yet again and
all seemed well. I climbed into the back of the car for a drive which
at that time of night should have taken twelve minutes at the most.
Gratefully I shut my eyes as we started off and when I opened them
again we were proceeding at a confident speed all right but my watch
told me that we had already been going for twenty-five minutes. It did
not look too good and I thought I had better take a more active
interest. I asked my driver if there was any problem and he assured
me that there was not such a thing, saying finally, 'Please do not
worry. It take five minutes.' We then began to turn corners at great
speed and I peered through the windows in the hope of spotting a
familiar landmark. Another five minutes passed and it became clear
that he had not the smallest idea where 143A New Muslim Town was.

I became a fraction more excited and he was giving me a 'Please do not worry. It take five minutes' about three times every thirty seconds. I suggested quite forcibly that the only hope was to go back to the Intercontinental, ask for the directions again and have another go. But that was not a hit with the driver and on we went.

I was rapidly approaching a high state of excitement as the conversation progressed in Urdu on the one hand and in English on the other without any mutual understanding whatever when I suddenly spotted an advertising sign which I knew was in New Muslim Town. The next problem was that none or almost none of the streets have their names up and although we were in the right district, New Muslim Town stretches over a considerable area and I was not substantially nearer my bed. We drove round and round and round in furious circles and I was still being assured 'It not take five minutes.' We had been going for more than an hour when I spotted a big sign which said Business Executive which I knew was at the top of the street. The louder I tried to persuade the driver to turn right the harder he pressed his foot on the accelerator and it was two blocks before I could persuade him to stop and turn round. Now we had to turn left and then it was past the small park on the right and on until we met the road works. Then I saw the house on the right and there we were. I cannot describe my relief as I paid off the driver and then turned to the gates into the small drive which were of course locked. Although this was natural, I had not thought of it and it came as a bit of a shock. So I hammered on the big metal gates and nothing happened. Something close to despair was beginning to set in when eventually I heard a stirring at the back of the house and shortly a bleary-eyed nightwatchman appeared and let me in. Mercifully, the keys to the front door were still in my pocket.

Ashraf the Elder called me the next morning with a thermos of black tea, some freshly squeezed orange juice and a copy of the *Pakistan Times*. I thought Sarfraz's statement had been thrown away on the back page. Even so, copy like 'the tirade of a madman under the influence of dope' and 'How could he perform well if he was drugged out of his mind?' made it look a trifle silly. In all the statement seemed even more muddled than it had the night before and I could not help but wonder, if it ever got that far, how Sarfraz would fare in the witness box. Later, when Ashraf the Elder had driven me to the Gadaffi Stadium, I walked out to the middle with Tony Lewis to have a look at the pitch and was summoned by Alan Smith who said he wanted to have a word with me. I agreed to join him in front of the pavilion fifteen minutes after the match began. Reactions in the press-box differed. Matthew Engel, who had handled the saga amusingly and brilliantly in the *Guardian*, was greatly amused. Johnny Woodcock kept shaking his head and saying 'Where do we go from here?' Peter Smith said he thought Sarfraz had been stupid. Robin Marlar was having a good laugh and Graham Otway thanked me for calling him and told me what had happened at his end at the Hilton. I then saw Alan Smith and told him exactly what had happened during the night including one or two comments it would be libellous even now to print. Alan, who was clearly having one hell of a time, thought he would talk to Sarfraz. While we were talking a fairly short, fit-looking middle-aged man in a yellow T-shirt attracted Alan's attention through the wire fence which separated the players' enclosure from the terracing. He thanked Alan for the call he had made that morning. It was Alan Herd, Botham's solicitor, whom Smith had rung first thing to advise him to read Sarfraz's statement. The only response purported to have come from Herd that morning was 'I wish my client would keep his something mouth shut.' Alan Smith was himself upset by Botham's offensive remarks about Pakistan and later in the day issued a statement refuting them in the strongest of terms.

It was a relief to get away from it all that evening when Tony Lewis and I had dinner with some of Majid Khan's friends. The floor was held by a former federal minister and his striking wife, also a politician in her own right, a substantial landowner and an outspoken feminist which was quite a combination. Various political discussions took place in a mixture of languages, one of which developed into a highly acrimonious debate. Majid took us both home dropping Tony first. To my delight I found that I had successfully worked out how to get back. It was left at the canal after leaving the stadium, first right over the bridge, immediately second left at the Marker Pharmaceuticals sign – there were two roads as close as tramlines – straight over at the Bata Shoes sign and right at the Business Executive sign, over one cross-roads, past the small park on the right, over another cross-roads and there it was on the right in front of the road works. I shall know it in twenty years time but then of course the road works will probably have gone and Sarfraz will have moved house.

As I say, all navigational aids worked and Sarfraz himself opened the door. Farooq was there and we settled down to talk although with Farooq there it was more a question of sitting down to listen, which for me is an unusual experience. But Farooq is always great value. The gist of the conversation was that Sarfraz wanted to know what to do next. During the day he had spoken to various people including his great friend Imran who had just returned from England, and I got the impression that he was having second thoughts about what he had said. He now told us that those whom he wanted to name as links in the chain were not prepared to come clean. Farooq said that did not matter as witnesses could be found. We were talking round in circles when the telephone rang in Sarfraz's bedroom. My host answered and returned to tell us that Ian Botham had issued a fulsome apology saying that his earlier remarks had been made while suffering from post-operative depression. Farooq said straightaway that as Sarfraz had got everything he wanted he should drop the whole thing. Sarfraz then said that everyone smokes pot and that it was nothing to do with him and he didn't mind. Farooq reminded him that he had made his original statement to uphold the honour of Pakistan and that with the apology the honour of the country had been satisfied. Sarfraz now volunteered that he would repeat all that he had originally said but that he would be unable to find the guy who had produced the hashish in the first place. Sarfraz had had massive second thoughts.

The following evening I was invited to dine in Majid's family house in Zamaan Park. The small park and all the splendid houses around it are owned by the family and after dinner on the way home Majid drove me round the area. It was a most impressive display of family solidarity. It is extraordinary too, that three sisters should all have produced captains of Pakistan: Javed Burki, Majid Khan and Imran Khan. It was sad that Majid's father and mother were away in Islamabad for I would have loved to have met his father, Jehangir Khan. After dinner we looked at his father's old photographs hanging round the walls. There were the first two official Indian sides to tour England, in 1932 and 1936. Jehangir is the only survivor of the first. There was also the photograph of the sparrow Jehangir had killed in flight while bowling to Tom Pearce for Cambridge against MCC at Lord's in 1938. The sparrow has been stuffed and mounted on the ball and is to be found in the Museum at Lord's.

Jehangir was a remarkable natural athlete and Majid told me an extraordinary story about him. When Jehangir was young he went one day to see a friend run in the inter-university sports in India. While watching, he wandered over onto the grass in the centre of the track and happened to pick up a javelin. He asked the chap in charge what it was for and when he had been told he asked if he could have a go. With his very first throw he beat the Indian all-comers' record. In the next few minutes precisely the same thing happened with the hammer and the shot. He went on to represent India in the Commonwealth Games with the javelin. It was during the course of the evening that some more of Majid's cousins, the Zamaans, promised to arrange a day's wild boar hunting for me on the rest day of the Test match.

That evening had an amusing ending when I got home. Again Majid dropped me and again my directions were word perfect and when we arrived outside Sarfraz's house, people were pouring out of another car parked in front of the gates. Sarfraz was there, so were the Shah brothers, the restaurant owners from Bradford, and also a tall silvery-haired man who remained silent in a slightly chilling way as he sat on the sofa while we all talked. The next day Sarfraz, as I thought, told me he was a Bulgarian. Farooq was of course among those present and he wasted no time in telling me what he had written in 'Gossiping Aloud', his column in the *Pakistan Times*. It was about the umpiring, some of which that day had been distinctly questionable. I was exhausted and at about midnight I left Farooq in mid-sentence and went to bed. I had been asleep for about an hour when suddenly I was woken up by the door being opened and the light was switched on. It was the Bulgarian looking a little bit the worse for wear. He strode straight past me into the bathroom despite my protestations and proceeded to have what I can only describe as a noisy pee. I was highly put out and told him to go somewhere else. He took no notice and when he had finished he walked back through my bedroom. I gave him a tremendous burst. He walked out of the room leaving the light on and the door open and I shouted after him to come back and shut it and for good measure added something about his being an ill-mannered bastard. Against the odds he came back, turned out the light and shut the door. But he had the last word an hour or two later when he left. Once again, he opened my door as noisily as possible and then for good measure he slammed it shut with a force which almost shook the pictures off the wall. Game, set and match. At first I thought his Bulgarian background probably explained his behaviour, but soon it transpired that I had got that wrong for Sarfraz explained, more slowly this time, that he was not so much a Bulgarian as a brigadier.

While this highly diverting week unfolded off the field in Lahore, England found themselves playing another Test. Now that Bob Willis and Graham Dilley had departed to England, they were down to the

barest possible minimum of twelve players. After bowling so well in
Faisalabad and looking as if he would redeem a most disappointing
tour, Dilley had found that he had lost all the feeling down one side
of his body and he returned urgently to London for further medical
advice. After an operation he was unable to play at all during the 1984
season in England. Meanwhile Bob Willis had been wandering around
looking the very picture of gloom and was clearly not well. A virus
was diagnosed which it was feared might be hepatitis, and he also flew
home and did not play for the first month of the English season
although he returned for the one-day matches and the Test series
against the West Indies.

David Gower stayed in charge, therefore, for the Third Test. Zaheer
Abbas won the toss for Pakistan and, prompted no doubt by Sarfraz,
put England into bat. This time they batted carelessly on a pitch which
did not have much in it for the bowlers even at the College End where
water had leaked under the covers two evenings earlier. England were
bowled out for 241 and they only got this far thanks to a determined
innings of 74 by Vic Marks who showed what could be done against
the leg breaks and googlies of Abdul Qadir if you took the trouble to
work out a logical method of playing him. Marks protected his stumps
on the principle that if the ball pitched to the off side of the middle
stump it was the googly which was turning into him and if it pitched
on the leg side it was the leg-break turning the other way. It may not
have been glamorous but it was effective. I asked Marks afterwards if
he thought he would ever be able to read Abdul Qadir. He answered
cheerfully, 'Not in a million years.' Marks is the most delightful of
men. In this innings he was given brave support by Fowler who batted
at number six. Pakistan did not fare much better and again bad batting
was the cause. Qasim Omar fought hard for 73, his best score of the
series, and on the third day there was a splendid partnership between
Zaheer, who had pulled a muscle in the field on the first day and
needed a runner, and Sarfraz who is no fool with the bat. By now the
pitch was very easy and these two put on 161 before Sarfraz was
caught at slip off Chris Smith's occasional off-breaks when ten short
of what would have been his first Test hundred. Zaheer finished with
82 not out and showed what a fine player he is against anything but
the highest pace.

England's second innings revolved round another marathon effort
by Gower who made 173 not out. Mike Gatting played well for 53
and once again Marks reached 50, his third in successive Test innings

and it was an innings of great character. Then, with half an hour's playing time left before lunch, Gower declared leaving Pakistan to score 243 in three hours and the twenty overs which have to be bowled in the last hour. The umpires decided that a minimum of 39 overs would have to be bowled before the last hour began. Pakistan were then given a superb start by Mohsin Khan and Shoaib Muhammad, the son of Hanif, the Little Master. They had 100 up in 32 overs which meant that Pakistan needed 139 to win from the last 27 overs which was by no means impossible. It had also looked as if England would get through significantly more than the minimum of 39 overs before the last hour began, especially as the spinners had a fair bit to do. Seeing this, Gower and his bowlers deliberately slowed down the game to an unacceptable level. Left-arm spinner Nick Cook sometimes took as long as five minutes to bowl an over as field placings were minutely adjusted and he had long conversations with his captain. Nowadays the laws are stretched to the limit by the players and to prevent this happening in the future umpires should be given powers to prevent it. There is no doubt that if England had bowled 45 or more overs in those three hours Pakistan would have won. As it was they should have won but they allowed themselves to panic in the final overs. After Shoaib had hit a full toss from Norman Cowans straight to short midwicket, five more wickets fell while 26 runs were scored with Cowans taking 5/15 in four overs, and by the end Pakistan were struggling to keep out England. England's time-wasting was hard to defend but even so Pakistan allowed themselves to panic in the closing stages when they had the match won. Mohsin reached a delightful hundred and Shoaib looked a most impressive chip off the old block. At all events, the draw enabled Pakistan to win their first ever series against England and it was a victory they fully deserved. It was just a pity that so much else had been happening to distract attention from the cricket itself.

14
Hunting Wild Boar

At dinner with Majid Khan that night in Zamaan Park I had met Hurmyun Zamaan, the eldest of the three brothers, who promised to arrange the wild boar hunt. He was a big man with a warm open face, a charming smile below a friendly moustache and was just what the Americans would describe as a 'lovely' man. One of his main hobbies in life was shooting wild boar and almost every weekend he and his brothers or friends would go out into the country in pursuit of the boar. He was obviously immensely fit. He and his brother Javed were going to take me early on the morning of the rest day to some scrub land owned by their uncle situated some forty-five miles south-west of Lahore. Javed was in his early forties and was still captain of the Gymkhana Cricket Club in Lahore where he told me he still picks up his three of four wickets with his off spinners each week. Like Hurmyun, he was an amusing, compelling extrovert and I knew that evening that I would have the most delightful day.

Two years before, these two had taken Dennis Lillee and Rodney Marsh on a boar hunt when they had been in Lahore during an Australian tour. They had gone down to some land about fifteen miles south of Lahore on the Indian border for a night shoot by searchlight, which I gathered was the most exciting way of hunting the boar, but the least productive. The people shooting, who use 12-bores, are driven around on the back of Land Rovers which also carry searchlights which temporarily blind the boar and in the best Hopalong Cassidy style the shooters open up. That night they did not see any boar, though Lillee and Marsh shot a number of rabbits. The boar are considered vermin in Pakistan for they destroy the crops and so are a public menace. Whenever a boar is killed its tail is cut off and the

Government pay seventy-five rupees for every tail. I believe the meat is delicious to eat but of course it is against the Muslim religion even to touch a pig, dead or alive. I heard that there were plans being made to export the boar meat to non-Muslim countries.

Hurmyun explained after dinner that although a night shoot is more dramatic, we would be much more likely to shoot a few boar during the day. I was told that we would stand while the rough birch and scrub were beaten towards us by beaters who came from the neighbouring villages and that I would almost certainly get some shooting.

The rest day was the Thursday and I had to be round at Javed Zamaan's house by 6.30 a.m. for breakfast before setting off at seven o'clock by Land Rover. The Zamaans were arranging for me to borrow a gun and I was asked whether I would like to use one with barrels which were under and over or side by side. I was not worried. Hurmyun then told me stories about his most exciting moments shooting boar and he warned me that he had several times been charged by boars which had been put up close to him. I asked him if we were likely to come across any snakes and he told me that it was very seldom that they came onto this land which was often flooded during the monsoon when the Ravi came over its banks. I gathered they were the sort which would kill you before their fangs were back in their mouths, but the possibility was so remote that it was not worth considering.

I went to bed early and set my alarm for 5.30 after telling Ashraf the Elder that I had to be at Javed Zamaan's house, which was directly opposite Imran's, at 6.30. I snatched my watch when I woke up and it said 6.22 which was a nasty shock. I cannot remember exactly what happened next, but by 6.32 I had shaved, dressed and was ready to go. But there was no sign of Ashraf the Elder and so I walked round to the back of the house and shouted his name. At first I flushed out only the old woman who was part of the entourage who cared for Sarfraz and also the delightful little girl of ten or eleven who always grinned from ear to ear whenever she saw me and kept repeating, 'Thank you very much' or 'I'm so sorry' which she had many times heard me say – indeed she made a very fair job of taking off my voice. I kept repeating Ashraf's name and they indicated that he was still in bed somewhere at the top of the outside staircase which went up at the back of the house. By gesturing I persuaded the young girl to run upstairs and wake Ashraf. The minutes were ticking away. I now waited by the front of the house peering anxiously down the passage

at the side praying that Ashraf would appear. By now five or six of
the staff had got up and were watching somewhat suspiciously from
a distance. I think it may have been my flat cap which made them all
a trifle apprehensive that morning. Eventually, at 6.45, a somewhat
flustered Ashraf the Elder appeared round the back of the house looking somewhat startled while patting his tummy and saying, 'Ill, ill.' He
may have had an upset tummy, but the main trouble probably was
that he thought I meant 6.30 p.m. and not 6.30 a.m. As it happened,
all was well for there was little traffic about and we drove into Javed
Zamaan's drive at 6.54.

There were two military-looking jeeps parked outside the house and
soon Javed appeared. He was in the best of form. Breakfast was the
first item on the agenda and apparently we were not all that hard
pressed for time. Hurmyun, who lived in another substantial Zamaan
Park house, had driven up to the land we were to shoot over an hour
before to arrange the final details. Javed introduced me to a large
friend who was coming to shoot with us, Mian Latif, who sold and
exported carpets and was the most delightful companion even if he cut
a slightly Beatrix Potterish sort of a figure. He wore a mauve kurti
kamise with a zip-up jacket on top. Breakfast was a veritable feast. I
started off with approximately a pint and a half of fresh orange juice.
Then I was offered corn flakes or, more remarkably, porridge which
Javed tucked into as if he was wearing a kilt underneath the table.
The Carpet King also went for the porridge. Next came quantities of
fried eggs and lovely warm chapatis. Finally, there was toast and
excellent honey, all of which was washed down with copious quantities
of coffee. By the time we clambered into the Land Rovers we were
ready for anything. It was decided over my head at breakfast that I
would borrow the Carpet King's side-by-side 12-bore and that he
would shoot with Javed's second under-and-over Russian gun which
I later discovered was beautifully balanced. The Carpet King's firing
piece was not quite so comfortable. The Carpet King took his jeep and
I was made to sit in the front while Javed stretched out, I hope not
too uncomfortably, in the back.

On the way out of Lahore we stopped at the telex office so that I
could file my stories for the day. Then we set off for the bush. Javed
pointed out the red-light district on the right as we went, but alas I
never had time to pay it a visit and add it to my considerable collec-
tion. Then it was across the Ravi and back down the Faisalabad road.
Soon we branched left onto the old Faisalabad road and drove for

some miles through suburbs. When we came to the open country little villages came thick and fast; the inhabitants were all making a start to the day which mostly meant standing around in groups by the side of the road and doing nothing very much. Besides the people, there were the usual ramshackle shops, every kind of animal wandering around and masses of excited children running all over the place except for those who were quite unselfconsciously squatting by the side of the road doing their daily after-breakfast stint.

We had been going for about an hour – the old road to Faisalabad contained as many brick kilns as the new road, belching black smoke at about half-mile intervals – when we turned sharp left just before a bridge over an enormous irrigation canal. We stopped immediately at a gate which barred our way onto the sandy road on top of the canal wall. A couple of bursts on the horn produced a gatekeeper who took one look at us and soon had it open. We must have driven along this road for seven or eight miles before another gate produced another halt. The same procedure applied and we drove on past a village made up of rather impressive mud huts. We now found we had come too far and returned almost to the gate and turned right down a narrow track which took us past the side of this village to another mud village which was surrounded by a huge mud wall. It was a rather more distinguished village and as we drove up to it I could see a substantial red-brick building in the middle. We skirted the village to the right and then we turned left following the wall. About fifty yards in front of us was a small squat one-roomed house built of brick and with pillars on either side of the front door. It was painted yellow and the two jeeps parked outside indicated that we had arrived and that this was the hunting lodge.

As we parked Hurmyun Zamaan came out of the lodge full of good cheer. We went inside and he told me that the land we were shooting over belonged to his uncle who would also be shooting. No sooner had he said this than two rather older men came through the door. One was the uncle who owned the land and had built the lodge. The other was his brother who had played hockey for Pakistan in the 1948 Olympics in London and had captained the Pakistan hockey team four years later in Helsinki, but he was not staying to shoot. The two of them had spent the night at the lodge. Hurmyun produced some formidably thick slices of bread and butter, and tea was dispensed and then it was time to start.

The Carpet King now gave me his gun and a pocketful of cartridges filled with buckshot for the boar take plenty of stopping. He, Javed and I piled back into the Land Rover and drove back the way we had come to the banks of the canal. The others were taking what Hurmyun called a 'short cut', but Hurmyun would have walked anywhere and as I later discovered the cut was not so very short. We followed the canal for a mile until it joined the Ravi at which point we turned left along the river, but after a few hundred yards we came to a very narrow irrigation canal which was no more than eighteen inches across and had been recently cut. It was just too wide for the Land Rover to cross and when one of the beaters jumped off to see how deep it was he found the water came up to his waist. We got out, jumped over the water and walked on for ten minutes until we came to a much wider irrigation canal which could only be crossed by boat. There was flat scrubland all around us where a few cattle were grazing and the river Ravi was flowing past us about ten yards to our right. Several big parties of duck flew overhead and landed on the mud flats on the other side of the Ravi which was all of half a mile across. The scrubland we were going to shoot lay across this second irrigation canal, but for the moment we could only wait for a boat to ferry us over.

But first the boat had to take across Hurmyun and his party of beaters some way up the canal where it was much wider. We had to wait for half an hour in which time the Carpet King fired vigorously at an enormously high goose which did a tail jink as polite recognition but otherwise proceeded without noticeable inconvenience. Eventually the small rowing boat reached us and we were lifted across in relays. While we had been waiting a mixed herd of cows and buffaloes came along the river bank to this wider canal and without any persuasion they went straight in and swam across to the other side with the boys who looked after them riding on their backs.

Getting out of the boat was a slightly wobbly problem and while we then walked along the side of the canal for another five minutes, Javed explained to me that the thousands of acres of scrubland on our right would be driven and counterdriven in blocks by the beaters with three of the five guns standing and the other two walking with the beaters. The scrub was mostly reed and birch and did not rise much above head height although it was tough walking in the heat for you could not walk normally but had to pick your back foot up after each step so that it did not get caught in scrub. We soon reached the point where Hurmyun and the others had disembarked and after shouting instructions to the beaters it was time to get down to the serious business of the day. Apparently the land in front of us with the canal on the left was going to be driven towards us and as there was a good chance that any boar there would follow the path alongside the canal, the Carpet King and I were stationed by Javed to cover that area. The others were I think a little uncertain as to my form with a gun and understandably they kept a careful eye on me. The Carpet King took up a position whith me in a slight dip with both a cross-path and the pathway which came down the side of the water converging in front of us. It was an excellent vantage point for it gave us good vision for shooting. The Carpet King now pulled up some tall green plants and strewed them around on the branches of a couple of small bushes in front of us to add to the camouflage and we waited. It was exciting.

After about ten minutes of suspense, Javed, who was standing about fifty yards to our right behind some more cover, suddenly shouted in Urdu to the Carpet King. There was quite a conversation and I thought I detected a note of surprise in their voices. The Carpet King then turned to me and told me that we had been facing the wrong way and that they were beating the land behind us and not the country in front. This put rather a different complexion on things, but there seemed to be no urgency and so we strode in leisurely fashion across the open ground in front and into the scrub on the other side where we soon found another vantage point. It was now clear that we had got it right this time for in the distance away to the left but in front of us all the same, we could hear the excited shouts of the beaters with whom Hurmyun and his uncle, the owner, were walking.

By now I had loaded my gun and was waiting eagerly for a boar to break cover when the peace was shattered by yells and screams and the barking of sundry dogs in the middle distance. The Carpet King and I crouched low and peered through the undergrowth. My thumb fidgeted restlessly with the safety catch. I held my gun at the ready and waited. Soon word came by means of the bush telegraph from the left that a herd of boar had been disturbed in front of us. It was all too good to be true. We waited at the ready for fully ten minutes. Then we stiffened as we heard more yells and screams from the beaters. These were followed at once by two shots in rapid succession from the same direction and more yelling. I crouched even lower with my right index finger curled round the front trigger waiting for the boars to burst out of the cover in front of us.

Distant shouts followed and the Carpet King was quick to interpret the dramas which had been unfolding in the middle distance. He

told me that Hurmyun had been charged by a huge boar which had
surprised him at close quarters. Hurmyun had fired instinctively as it
had charged him and had then missed again after it had left him. He
was unhurt and, knowing Hurmyun, revelling in it all. I was digesting
this when Javed on our left stood up and shouted and waved, pointing
far away to his left flank. 'We must move quickly' he shouted and set
off at the double. The Carpet King now showed a turn of speed his
ample figure did not suggest and I set off with him after emptying my
gun. We half-walked and half-ran for at least half a mile through the
scrub and it was hot work. The Carpet King suddenly took a short
cut and veered off to the right while I dogged Javed's footsteps. The
Carpet King ended up about a hundred yards further on than the two
of us. We stood together in some open ground at the corner of this
vast area of scrub. One of our objects was to prevent the boars inside
this piece of scrub from daring to cross the open ground to more
scrubland behind us. We had been there only a minute or two when
yells and waving of arms – we could see the beaters now in the middle
distance – were followed by a single shot and even more yells which
told us that contact had been re-established with the enemy in either
the singular or the plural.

There was now more shouting in Urdu and Javed waved and said
something in Urdu to the Carpet King with the result that to my
amazement we set off again at the double in precisely the direction we
had just come from. There was not a cloud in the sky and it was
oppressively hot. Apart from the daily trek from my bedroom to the
dining room and back, I was conspicuously short of exercise and very
unfit. Anyway, Javed and I arrived back at our original positions and
I was glad to see that we had set too hot a pace for the Carpet King.
I immediately reassumed a pose of hostile readiness. We waited for a
short time before the classic formula for wild boar hunting, which I
was quickly picking up, repeated itself. First came the yells, then the
shots followed quickly by rumours that Hurmyun had been charged a
second time, and finally the shout and wave from Javed indicating that
it was time to return to the spot we had just left and where the Carpet
King had taken up more or less permanent residence. This time we
had gone about half-way at a pace which had, I am afraid, fallen to
a slow-medium walk when Javed, who was just ahead of me, jumped
up and down, pointed and shouted, 'Look, look, a boar running over
the open ground.' I was at his side in a moment and peering hopefully
in the direction he was pointing. I could not see anything that remotely

resembled a boar, moving or stationary, but I did not want to let the side down and I said 'Yes, yes' knowingly and with considerable excitement and nodded my head a couple of times. Now we quickened our step to a slow-medium trot and, breathless, arrived at our old position where we waited in vain while the scrub in front of us was beaten out. After that, Hurmyun, who was greatly excited, gave a highly entertaining blow-by-blow account of his battle with the charging boar.

Already I was half-way to being exhausted and it seemed to me that I had come without the one essential for wild boar hunting, namely a pair of running shoes. But Hurmyun had really got the bit between his teeth and there was no letting up. I was given a quick glass of water out of a thermos carried by one of the beaters while Hurmyun's uncle had a cup of hot tea from another. At that moment I could not help thinking back to shoots at home in Norfolk when one felt surreptitiously into one's pocket for a hip flask and had a crafty swig of brandy or whisky which was what I needed now. I badly wanted some extra power from somewhere.

We set off in groups across the open ground to the scrub which had been behind us and into which Javed's running boar had disappeared. I was walking with Javed on the left and as we entered the scrub, he suddenly stopped and pointed again shouting, 'Look, a partridge.' Again, I strained my eyes with considerable enthusiasm, but could see nothing. 'It landed over there,' he said before I had a chance to say that I had not seen it. Now, partridges were out of season, but it was agreed between Javed and the Carpet King who was on my right that laws were made for breaking occasionally. I was going to be allowed the privilege of shooting it. The Carpet King sent over a beater with two cartridges which contained number eight shot and so I removed the buckshot from my gun and popped them in. Javed also put in a couple of number eights and with two beaters between us we walked stealthily forward into the slight dip where Javed had seen the partridge land. I could see the ghastly moment fast approaching when I was going to have to make a fool of myself. I advanced steadily with my gun at the ready. There was a rustling noise to my left followed by a shout and the partridge got up much nearer to Javed than me. I thought, 'Thank goodness for that. I won't have to do anything about it.' But nothing happened and it occurred to me that he was leaving it for me. I hurriedly brought my gun up to my shoulder and by now the partridge was some way off. As my finger tightened round the trigger I think the bird must have looked under its wing and was so appalled at what it saw that it instantly had a heart attack. I managed to get my gun off to make it look as if it was for real and everyone was congratulating me. It had fallen into a pool of water and a beater retrieved it and brought it to Javed. It was the unluckiest partridge in the whole of the Punjab. Javed now took it from the beater, got out his pen knife and slit the throat of the bird from side to side. I asked him what on earth he was doing and he said simply, 'It is our religion.' I assumed, maybe naïvely, that it was done to let out the spirit.

At all events my stock was now sky high with the beaters as we continued across the scrubland. Not long after that another partridge was put up on the right and it landed a couple of hundred yards ahead of Javed and I in another low-lying piece of ground. More cartridges with number 8 shot were distributed – cartridges cost a small fortune in Pakistan – and we surrounded the area. There was no escape for this partridge. Dogs and intrepid beaters went to work and eventually the partridge spiralled up into the air. It was very much a slow-medium partridge too, and in fact I don't think I have ever seen a partridge fly so slowly. I had first go at it and loosed off twice without touching a feather. I felt a complete idiot, but my state of being improved when six other shots were fired at it with precisely the same effect. As if to rub it in, the partridge landed only about 200 yards away. Hurmyun and I went after it, but it obviously ran and we never saw it again.

By now it was half-past twelve and we had been on the go for more than three hours. It was unbelievably hot and sticky but mercifully we all gathered in a group and waited for a moment or two before, quite miraculously, a panni wallah arrived. A young man came strutting towards us from the vague direction of the village where we had all foregathered which I discovered was called Kila Korka. He had a small piece of rag wrapped round in a circle on the top of his head and on top of that was balancing a large aluminium pot full of cold water. He walked as fast and as energetically as he would have done if he had had only a hat on his head. I asked Javed if the water would be OK for a Western stomach and he told me that it was beautifully pure and came from an artesian well in the village just outside the lodge. We all gulped down the most delicious water, beaters and all, while Hurmyun's uncle had another go at his hot tea.

Then it was time to go on, but now at least we were walking back towards home. Even so the scrubland between the jeep and ourselves seemed to stretch for miles. We were all feeling weary except of course for Hurmyun who might have been just beginning the day. He was first to his feet and led the way. Javed and I were the last to leave and this time we stayed on the right of the line as the beaters, encouraged by Hurmyun, began an enormous sweeping movement on the left. Javed and I walked for a few yards and then stopped to talk and we carried on like this for a while, stopping and starting. Eventually, he suggested that we should stay where we were as we had arrived at the point where this particular drive ended when the beaters came round to complete the circle. We had a marvellous coffee-house session talking about anything and everything. After a while, at his suggestion, we moved up to our right and as we walked conversation turned to cricket. Javed was himself an off-spinning all-rounder who had been having a good season with the Lahore Gymkhana. When we stopped we were talking about Imran and his leg injury and whether he would ever be able to bowl fast again when behind Javed there was a sudden rustling sound in the reeds. He spun round and I looked over his shoulder and we saw two boar burst out of the scrub into the open about twenty yards away. They moved like lightning and looked horribly fierce although they were a little smaller than I had anticipated. As Javed spun round he seemed to fire as if from the hip while I was much too slow and in any event would have been more likely to have shot my host than a boar for he was standing in front of me. Javed's shooting was brilliant for a violent kicking in the reeds showed that he had scored a direct hit. We ran across and there was a boar in its final death throes and the spreading blood stain on the beast's flank showed that it had been a perfect shot hitting the boar in the heart just behind the front legs. It is not often that one shot is enough to kill these animals. Javed was overjoyed and the two beaters with us jumped up and down with delight and beaters came running from the far distance to have a look. Anyone would have thought that World War III had been won, but the villagers detest these animals for they destroy such a large part of the crops. They had good reason to dance round the corpse. After a time a beater stepped forward with a small axe and chopped off a rather mangy tail. An older man then produced a piece of reed which he folded into a big V-shape in order to pick up the tail without touching it which would have been against the Muslim religion and would have brought evil spirits down on him. Before leaving the body, which would be eaten by jackals or other boars who are cannibals, I was shown the tusks which were venomous-looking objects about two inches long. Unfortunately my camera was in a bag being carried by the beater with the thermos who had not run over to join in the last rites.

Eventually order returned and we set off again. Action was now thick and fast as yelping dogs told us there were more boar about and I soon found myself running from place to place even faster than I had done in the first part of the day. There were intermittent shots and the Carpet King probably had the best chance of making another kill. We also saw a jackal or two. Hurmyun was still as keen as ever to walk for miles more. At last we came to the canal where we had started shooting in the morning. We walked a wide section of the scrub which had been driven towards us at the start, down towards the river. We had been walking for about ten minutes when it all began again. The dogs barked, the beaters yelled and two shots were fired in rapid succession and then a third. More yells and general jubilation told us that another boar had been killed. Hurmyun had been the executioner and for the third time that day he had been charged. It was a big animal and he had killed it with his third shot, but not before it had charged and gored a small boy who was with the beaters.

Hurmyun's account of the battle must have been even more dramatic than the encounter itself. In a state of great excitement he told us that the dogs had barked and that he thought he had seen the boar lying in a thicket ahead of him and he fired at it. But what he had thought was a boar was actually a lump of earth and the boar now charged at him from another part of the thicket. Hurmyun fired and hit it with his second shot, but the boar changed direction and charged at the boy, catching him a nasty blow on the thigh with one of its tusks. Hurmyun reloaded and proceeded to kill the boar with his third shot. The boy, who cannot have been more than twelve or thirteen, was as brave as anything and another beater tied a piece of cloth tight round his thigh to check the bleeding and cover the gash. The boy was unmoved.

It was all accepted as a matter of course. After we had posed for masses of photographs, the tail was cut off and reeds were plaited round it so that it could be carried. It was a huge male boar – I was told that they are forced to live on their own because they are so bad-tempered and disrupt the life of a herd. The injured boy now took a big stick from one of the other beaters and, watched by everyone, proceeded to flog the body of the dead animal as hard as he could. His face was full of hatred, and he must have delivered at least a dozen blows on its body, each one containing every ounce of his strength. The others stood and watched as though it was normal practice and these few moments showed me exactly how the villagers regarded these animals. I never discovered whether the beating was ritual and if it had a religious significance. Somehow it was an intensely private and personal moment which in its strange, rather macabre way was full of great strength and meaning and it would have been impertinent to question it. The name of the boy was Alladitta which means God Given, and after relieving his feelings he continued to act as a beater as we covered the remaining scrub between us and the river.

The rowing boat took us back over the canal and we walked to the Land Rover, but Hurmyun and his uncle had decided to walk home and to look for another boar on the way. Javed, the Carpet King and I, together with several beaters including Alladitta, jumped aboard the Land Rover and when we reached the first village alongside the main irrigation canal, the boy jumped off and walked up the hill to a mud house where there was a 'doctor'. None of the other beaters were in the least concerned. Back at the lodge we drank more water, cleaned the guns and sat down for an hour while waiting for the others to return. Hurmyun was pleased when they got back for they had killed another boar on the way home and again it was a joy to listen to his description of the kill. After that we had an excellent lunch of chicken curry, chapati and rice and by now I found that I had become quite good at eating with a combination of chapati and fingers for knives and forks were not used. I was given the partridge, which had been plucked and put into a bag, and the Carpet King, Javed and I got back into the Land Rover and drove back to Lahore. Along the way we drove off the road in a small village and stopped at a shop for some 7-Up and for three mango ice-creams which were delicious. The firm which made them was, appropriately enough, called Yummy's and I wondered if there had ever been a better name for an ice-cream. The advertisement, which was plastered everywhere, said simply, 'It's the Yummiest.' I can tell you it was even better than that.

By the time I got back to Sarfraz's house with my dead partridge I was exhausted, but I could not remember a day which I had spent anywhere in the world which I had found more interesting and which I had enjoyed more.

15

Relaxing on Rhodes

We had three days back at the Sheraton in Karachi and England beat Pakistan in the second of the two one-day internationals. Once again and contrary to rumour the students, who have an almost unblemished record for stopping international matches at the National Stadium by rioting, hardly flexed their muscles. It was not an especially big crowd although during the afternoon several canisters of orange smoke were thrown into one of the stands which was crowded and cleared it in a matter of moments. This match was played on the Monday and it was an early start on the Tuesday morning for Heathrow by kind permission of British Airways. After eight nights in England it was another early start, this time from Gatwick for a flight to the island of Rhodes and then the fifty minutes drive to the village of Lindos. I planned to spend three weeks there in order first of all to charge the batteries in a house perched underneath the acropolis and overlooking one of nature's more spectacular bays, and then to dredge through my winter's travels and write this book. Even after almost six months of dashing to airports and frantic and largely unsuccessful attempts to make my clothes fit inside my cases, the adrenalin was still there as I bought my train ticket that morning from Victoria to Gatwick just after half-past five.

Lindos was only just emerging from its five months of winter hibernation. At the end of October, as soon as the last drachma has been rung through the tills and the last tourist has caught his taxi to Rhodes airport, the shutters come down. The locals and the few expatriates who have their homes in this lovely village then batten down the hatches for the winter and the bar and restaurant owners and all those who have been making money by the sackful during the summer months fly away to spend it. Those who have been serving retsina and ouzo or moussaka and taramasalata and kebabs for seven months and those who have been trying to assist the unathletic to water-ski with a charm which is unfailing, although it can grow a trifle strained by the end of the season, simply pack their bags and beat it.

The indomitable Socrates (with a long 'a' as in cart) closes his bar with a flourish, downs his last tequila bang-bang, turns off the record player and departs – at least he did last year – for Goa. Manolis Pallas boards up the Acropolis disco and sits reflectively in his travel agency until London or New York beckon, while his brother Dimitri packs away the tables which have adorned the Pallas beach since April and locks the front door of his taverna. His heads for Europe. Dimitri Mavrikos closes the iron gates in front of Mavrikos restaurant in the square and with his Norwegian wife Anna and baby Vassilios they depart for Oslo. Steffan and Maggie tidy up Hermes, sister restaurant to Magno's in London's Long Acre. Alexis and Sally bang the door on the Apollo bar and their jewellery shop too. Jenny May makes sure that the Jenny May Travel villas are left in ship-shape condition. And so it goes on. Yannis and Sofia in the supermarket are two who get less rest for they stay open to cope with the needs of those who winter in Lindos, and Yannis is busy running the affairs of Lardos, a neighbouring village where he lives. They are interrupted only by the clacking of an occasional typewriter by a would-be author who has holed himself up for the winter to put it all on paper.

Wednesday 4 April is the first day of the new season. As I jump out of my taxi in the square, Dimitri waves to me from the entrance to Mavrikos resturant, Manolis Pallas is there to share the first bottle of wine produced by Leftheric who has got himself engaged to a stunning girl and then Socrates booms in. He is opening his bar that night. Jenny May appears for I am her first customer of the year and all of a sudden I feel as though I have never been away. I suppose it is the same when you return to any familiar place after a longish absence. Over the next few days the nearest I came to a cricket conversation was when an expatriate Englishman said he had heard me on the ether the other day from some strange part of the world. I suppose he had been listening to the World Service of the BBC. Each Wednesday Lindos is topped up with new arrivals and as my stay went on I began to get a few comments like 'Bit different then from Pakistan this.' By the time I left the English papers, which arrive a day late, had reported that Leicestershire had beaten Cambridge University by 522 runs and

I knew that it was about time to go. The book to this point was almost finished and next Saturday I was to watch Hampshire play Essex at Southampton for the BBC. All my best memories of the winter months were already down on paper in the pages you have read. All except one, and I only remembered it in Lindos because of an extraordinarily tall man who came one evening into Socrates' bar and sat down to play backgammon with his tiny girl friend.

In Sydney one day in January there had been no cricket and many of the players, including the West Indians and many of the commentators, had been invited to Kerry Packer's magnificent beach house at Palm Beach just outside Sydney. Joel Garner was standing on the beach with a drink in his hand when two small but very beautiful girls came up to him.

'May we ask you a question?' the first one asked.

'Of course,' came the reply.

'Would you mind telling us how tall you are?' she asked.

'Certainly,' Joel answered, 'I am six foot eight.'

The smaller of the two girls now joined in and asked him if she could ask him a question.

'Of course you can,' he replied.

'In which case will you tell us if the rest of your body is built in proportion to your height?'

'Good God, no,' came the horrified answer. 'If it was I should be thirteen foot six.'

My last weekend in Lindos took place on a somewhat different note for it was the Greek Easter, the first in which I had been involved. And it was quite an adventure. Unfortunately by now the village was full of tourists with hardly a room to be had and the religious ceremonies were sadly dominated by flashing cameras, a blabbering Babel of languages and clothes not normally worn on deeply religious occasions. The charming ceremonies could not help therefore being given the feel of tourist productions. It all began in the tiny medieval church in the middle of the village at half-past eight on Good Friday evening with the Epitaph. After a church service which we did not attend but stood outside by one of the bars, a procession of clergy and congregation set off round the village. As soon as the service ended, the procession, headed by a coffin covered in flowers and candles and followed by the priest, started through the streets before returning after half an hour to the church. The coffin was of course symbolic of the dead Christ.

The Easter Day festivities began with a splendid dinner at which we were all given hard-boiled eggs with coloured shells and candles. It was eleven o'clock when we ventured into the packed church where there was incessant chanting which was both mournful and rather tuneful. There was a mixture of locals and tourists standing crammed together in the centre of the building for the old stalls round the side had long since been filled. It was a smoky, hazy atmosphere for almost everyone bought and then lit candles which were placed in massive and multiple candle holders. I could not help smiling at the old ladies who presided over the candles for after one had been burning for ten minutes it was put out and sold to someone else and lit again. It was a charming service and I only wish I could have understood the language. Then midnight arrived and the priest processed out of the church, circled it once and then beat on the door asking in a loud voice if he had risen. Twice he was given the answer no and then the third time it was yes and the doors were flung open and pandemonium broke loose. Rockets were let off, people cheered and everyone lit their candles. The idea was to return home with them still alight, but by now a considerable wind had got up and most like mine were blown out within ten yards of leaving the church. Some of the restaurants now served Easter food, but we were unable to find one with an empty table and so went back home to celebrate. The best of the festival food came the next day for it is the Greek custom the day after Easter to roast whole sheep on the spit. At the back of his taverna, Dimitris Pallas roasted five and I have never tasted better mutton in my life.

Two days later it was back to Rhodes airport for the flight to Gatwick, and the awful actuality of real life. But what a winter it had been and what a way to finish it off too! I came back to London ready for anything; yes, even for annihilation by the West Indies. It had all been such fun.

16
The Mixture As Before

It was back from Lindos on the Wednesday evening and into real life on Saturday when Graham Gooch, one of those banned by England for three years for having taken part in the South African Breweries tour of South Africa, hit 200 for Essex against Hampshire at Southampton. The events of the next twelve months were quick to unwind. The West Indies beat Australia 3–0 in the Caribbean and probably it should have been 5–0. After the final Test match in Kingston the West Indians leapt onto an aeroplane and within days had begun to demolish England. They showed a brief flicker of mortality at Trent Bridge when they lost a one-day international, but went on to win that particular series by two matches to one.

The Test series was about as one-sided as any can ever have been and the West Indies won all five matches without ever suggesting it would be any different. After Viv Richards's staggering 189 in the first one-day international at Old Trafford he had, by his standards, a poor summer and after that early match the others took it in turn. Larry Gomes, as determined as ever, hit hundreds, Gordon Greenidge won the Lord's Test with a prodigious 214 not out on the last day, Malcolm Marshall destroyed England at Headingley with his left hand in a plaster cast, Michael Holding eventually went back to his long run, Clive Lloyd made batting seem even easier than ever and on it went.

Poor David Gower in his first full series as England's captain did a number of things right, but his own form with the bat was no help and he was short of raw materials. Allan Lamb had an extraordinary summer scoring three hundreds in the Test matches against the West Indies, which is an even more remarkable achievement when the opposition wins all five. Paul Downton, who had taken over behind the stumps when the selectors decided that Bob Taylor's days were over, showed any amount of guts and a correct technique with the bat while Pat Pocock's off-spin was back in favour before the end of the summer and the two openers, Graeme Fowler and Chris Broad, had shown that they were as brave as lions. Bob Willis bowled his heart out in his final Test series taking his tally of wickets in Test cricket to 325. England emerged with something on the credit side, therefore, although Ian Botham did not have a good series and announced during the Fourth Test at Old Trafford that he was going to spend the winter at home and would not be available for the tour of India.

Botham had probably been Gower's greatest single problem. He is headstrong and difficult to captain for he tends to ignore his skipper and do as he wants. He seldom allowed Gower to take him off and maybe, too, he seized the ball when he felt he wanted to bowl. Gower did not perhaps feel that his own authority was well enough established for him to take on his leading player. When Gower had captained England in those two Test matches in Pakistan, Botham had already flown home with a knee injury. To bring the best out in Botham as a player, he needs to be disciplined by his captain. Mike Brearley understood this although the two of them had many disagreements; Willis did not and Gower has learned the hard way. A significant incident during the English summer was the appearance of the former South African all-rounder, Eddie Barlow, in London where he took up his appointment as South Africa's ambassador for sport. He is a known opponent of apartheid who has stood for parliament in opposition to the Nationalist party, but he takes the view that the time to end the sporting isolation of South Africa has arrived. Isolationism, he feels, is a negative policy with no constructive thoughts behind it and ends up harming those whom it is setting out to protect, namely the non-European races. In my view he has an impossible task ahead of him if he is to try and convince the dedicated opponents of South Africa, who will see this as a backdoor method of allowing South Africa once again into open competition round the sporting world. But Barlow is a tough man and he will not fail for want of trying. It was nice to see him at the Test matches.

The West Indians went their various ways after the Fifth Test at the Oval in early September and the delightful Sri Lankans took their place. They played some rather patchy cricket in a few games against the counties before coming to Lord's for their first-ever Test Match in England. What a surprise they caused. Gower put them in, a trifle patronisingly perhaps, and watched them score 474 for 9 declared against bowlers who were still suffering from a West Indian hangover. One of their openers, Sidath Wettimuny, finally dispensed with the theory that Sri Lankan batsmen, for all their natural brilliance, are unable to play the long innings which is necessary to win a Test Match. He made 193 and then his captain Duleep Mendis hit 111 in as exciting an innings as Lord's can have seen in a Test Match. Botham was sure he could bounce him out and Mendis kept hooking him into the old tavern area for six. England then went in and Lamb hit his fourth Test hundred of the summer. By now time was running short and Sri Lanka batted out the match with Mendis failing by only six runs to become the second batsman ever to hit a hundred in each innings of a Test Match at Lord's. The West Indian, George Headley, is the only man ever to have done it. The left handed Amal Silva also made a hundred in the second innings of a match which ended as a technical knock-out for England. In the BBC commentary box we were lucky enough to be able to call upon the services of Gamini Goonesena, the former Cambridge batsman who also bowled his leg breaks for Nottinghamshire and Sri Lanka and who has been living in Australia. He had a penchant for disappearing and bringing back into the box Sri Lankan Cabinet Ministers, who always had interesting views.

This match ended in early September and by the end of the month the programme planned for the other parts of the world during the English winter had already begun. New Zealand were having trouble with the umpires in Pakistan, the England selectors had chosen their party for India which included the orthodox left-arm spinner Phil Edmonds who in spite of a reputation for being a difficult man to handle had fought his way back into the side, and the West Indies had named their squad for Australia. When these series were over and Pakistan had visited New Zealand, all seven Test playing countries were to foregather in Melbourne for the so-called World Championship of Cricket which was being held as part of the celebrations for the 150th Anniversary of the founding of the State of Victoria. It was a six-month period which promised plenty of interest and excitement and also a fair amount of the drama which seems increasingly to accompany international cricket these days. As you have seen, the 1983/84 season was a good illustration of what I mean.

As usual, I watched and read about it all from the confines of the five Australian Capital Cities in the south of the country while the

West Indians slugged it out with Australia before Sri Lanka flew across the Indian Ocean to make the third side for the Benson & Hedges World Series Cup. The cricket in Australia itself was predictable enough, with the West Indies winning the Test series and the World Series Cup. Clive Lloyd's side won the first three Tests, taking their consecutive winning sequence to eleven matches – which is a record – before the captain delayed his declaration too long in the Fourth Test in Melbourne and Australia escaped with an uncomfortable draw. In Sydney, where New South Wales had spun themselves to victory over the West Indies in November, another spinner's pitch was produced which I am not sure would have stood up to a steward's enquiry and the same two spinners, Bob Holland and Murray Bennett, bowled Australia to victory by an innings and 55 runs.

This last match was Lloyd's final Test for he had decided, this time irrevocably, to retire from Test cricket at the end of the tour. He had resigned from the captaincy once before, after India had beaten the West Indies in the 1983 World Cup final at Lord's, but he had been persuaded to think again by the West Indies Board of Control. Now, on the fourth day with the West Indies second innings already in ruins at 46 for 3, Lloyd shuffled to the wicket in that slightly stooping way of his while the 24,000 spectators stood all the way round the ground and cheered him to the echo. Lloyd as always played watchfully, pensively and easily, thumping the odd ball away to the mid-wicket boundary and once advancing to drive Bennett over mid on and deep into the Hill. He leant comfortably into an off drive which went past extra cover for the two which took him to his fifty and suddenly it looked as if he might after all hit a century in a Test Match at the Sydney cricket ground – which is the only Test ground in Australia where this feat had eluded him.

A scything cut off Craig McDermott, Australia's newest star, took him into the sixties. Moments later a spanking extra cover drive brought him four more and then he drove again and this time edged McDermott for four. Lloyd was still chewing rhythmically and lugubriously as McDermott bowled him a yorker which he somehow dug out and just avoided playing the ball into his stumps. As he stepped away from his wicket, he held up his hand in a quick gesture of appreciation to the bowler from a man who has always been a generous opponent. I hope McDermott appreciated this but he is in danger of becoming a headstrong young man who seems to have trained on in the mould of Lillee and Lawson and the nuance probably escaped him. His next ball to Lloyd was almost but not quite a half volley and Lloyd unfurled another drive. This time he was not quite to the pitch and Border took the catch low down at extra cover. Lloyd shuffled off a Test ground for the last time to another standing ovation and on into the West Indian dressing room and the pages of the history books.

During the World Series Cup the Sri Lankans showed that the truth about their cricket is that while they have many highly talented players, they suffer from a lack of efficiency as a result of having no domestic first-class competition in which to hone their skills. They are not really battle-hardened and there is a damaging lack of efficiency about so much of their cricket. With the notable exceptions of Roy Dias and Aravinda de Silva there is a disappointing inconsistency about their batting. The batsmen are mostly very correct, which says a lot for the coaching system on the island, but as individuals they do not have enough exposure at the top level. If all the Sri Lankan Test cricketers were able to play a full season's county cricket, for example, they would improve immeasurably. As it is, all the other Test playing countries should entertain Sri Lanka or visit the island as frequently as they can if Test cricket's newest recruits are to learn to hold their own.

The amateur spirit of Sri Lankan cricket which is visible in the batting is even more noticeable in the bowling and fielding. Although they produce big men like Vinodhan John and Rumesh Ratnayake, none of them bowl genuinely fast and this is a big handicap when it comes to playing Test cricket, as India have so often found over the years. Conditions in Sri Lanka favour spin but at the moment, judging from the evidence of their players in Australia, they are also short of good class spinners. The raw materials must surely be there in a country which has produced so many fine natural players and the answer is first to find more and then to make sure they develop this natural ability with hard work and dedication. It is no good Sri Lanka making 239 for 7 in 50 overs against Australia as they did in their first match of the competition and then bowling a total of fifteen no-balls and wides thereby making Australia a present of two-and-a-half overs. As it happened, after taking these overs into account, Australia won with sixteen balls to spare. Bowlers who are short of pace but are forced to open the bowling must do their best to make up for it by tight control and this also only comes from hard work. As it was, in the World Series Cup their seam bowlers were hopelessly wayward in both length and direction. In the field too, a side which will struggle to bowl out its opponents must hold all its catches, but they fielded badly and practice is the only way this can be improved. A more demanding domestic competition in the island is a necessity.

For all that, Sri Lanka did well to win one match against Australia and it was only towards the end of the preliminary round that their bowling was shown up for what it was worth. Their players will return home wiser men and if they can learn the lessons Sri Lankan cricket will be better for the experience. The best-of-three finals for the World Series Cup found the West Indians suffering from the effects of cumulative tiredness towards the end of a programme of Test and international cricket which stretched back to September 1983 when Lloyd's side arrived in India. In the first match at the Sydney Cricket Ground they allowed Australia to recover from 64 for 4 to 241 for 7 although Border played one of the few memorable innings I have seen in one-day cricket making 127 not out. The West Indian batsmen, like the bowlers, found concentration hard to come by and they lost by 26 runs.

The West Indian lethargy spilled over to Melbourne where as usual Lloyd put Australia in and watched them amass 271 for 7 with Garner and Marshall giving away 60 and 64 runs respectively. It looked at the interval as if Australia would win the finals in straight matches, but during the break something happened in the West Indian dressing room. Their batsmen came out altogether more determined than they had been in Sydney and they were given a good start by Haynes, Richardson and Gomes, but Richards and Lloyd then went cheaply and the West Indies were 179/5 in the 37th over needing 93 from thirteen overs. If Richie Benaud, Ian Chappell or Bill Lawry had been captaining Australia, I doubt the West Indies would have won. Border now seemed to lose control against a magnificent onslaught by Logie and Dujon. They put on 86 in twelve overs before Logie hit his own wicket off the last ball of the 49th over. Seven were needed from the last over and Dujon drove Hogg's first two balls through and over extra cover to the boundary and the West Indian players in the pavilion ran on to the ground to congratulate him. The third final was a much more sedate affair with the West Indies back in control having got a second wind. The Australians, put in once again, made 178 with Holding bowling beautifully for 5/26 in his ten overs and Garner taking two stupendous catches, one at backward point and the other off his own bowling. Richards and Haynes then steered the West Indies to a most competent if unspectacular victory.

By this stage of the season a new Australia side was beginning to emerge under Border's rather stereotyped leadership. Back in November Australia's situation had looked hopeless when they lost the first two Tests, for there were no replacements around. But as the domestic season wore on, some young players made their mark. Craig McDermott, who was only nineteen, was one of the first to be called up and although he is still rather undisciplined in his approach and action, he is already capable of genuine pace. He is a marvellous find for he is a strapping young man who when he thickens out more will be unpleasantly fast. Simon O'Donnell, the young Victorian all-rounder – Australia has suffered badly from a shortage of all-rounders – also found a place and he improved both as a batsman and a bowler as the one-day series went on. To start with he was too committed for comfort to the front foot, but he learned fast. Another Victorian, Dean Jones, who had toured the West Indies with limited success, came back into the side and is a fine stroke-maker, who also favours the front foot, and a brilliant fielder. Steve Smith, the New South Wales opener, was another who was brought back and he improved the fielding too although he is a better limited over player than Test cricketer. He was most unlucky to break a finger fielding in the second of the finals. Robbie Kerr, another Queenslander, played towards the end of the season and made a big impact when Australia met England in the opening match for the World Championship of Cricket. By then Ritchie, also from Queensland, and Boon from Tasmania had been tried in the middle of the order and had been found wanting. By the end of the summer the future of Australian cricket looked much more assured than had seemed possible at the start. Most of these newcomers will have an important part to play.

While all this had been going on in Australia, England had been fully employed in India. A few hours after they had arrived in Delhi, Mrs Gandhi had been gunned down in her own garden by Sikh members of her bodyguard and for the next two days the side was marooned in its hotel as a wave of vengeance overtook Delhi. An extemporary visit to Sri Lanka was hastily arranged in the hope that after a few days the violence would quieten down. In Colombo England's main problem was the wet weather but the practice was useful and when the side returned to the mainland, life was quieter and they began a rearranged tour programme. But the dramas continued most unpleasantly when they reached Bombay for the First Test Match. A day or two before it began, the team went to a party at the house of the assistant British High Commissioner, Percy Norris, who was a very popular figure. The next morning, while he was being driven to his office, Mr Norris was shot and killed. Once again the future of the tour was in doubt, but the management decided that the First Test should go ahead as planned. The England players were not all convinced that this was right and they were well beaten by India. It is always a gloomy moment for a touring side when it loses the first Test of a series in India for it is not often that it will be given the chance to get back into the series.

England managed to level the series in the Second Test in Delhi, however, where opener Tim Robinson made 160 in only his second Test. England built up a first-innings lead of 111 and the spin of Edmonds and Pocock was too much for India in their second innings. After India's defeat Kapil Dev was dropped for the Third Test in Calcutta for 'irresponsible batting' during the Second, although it may have had more to do with his poor relations with his captain, Sunny Gavaskar. It caused a great public outcry but the selectors stood firm. The Third Test was a high-scoring draw and Kapil Dev was reinstated for the Fourth in Madras. Neil Foster came into the England side for the first time there on a pitch which in recent years has suited fast bowlers. Andy Roberts has bowled well at Chepauk for the West Indies and in 1976/77 John Lever did a good job for England in a match which was made famous by the 'vaseline incident'. With advice from Bernard Thomas, the England physiotherapist, Lever had stuck strips of vaseline impregnated gauze along his eyebrows to stop sweat trickling down into and stinging his eyes. As he frequently used the sweat from his brow to help polish the ball inevitably a certain amount of vaseline which would have helped the process found its way on to the ball. The umpires felt it was being used deliberately and it caused a minor furore until Tony Greig skilfully defused the issue at a press conference on the morning of the rest day. He advised the Indian journalists not to waste their time pursuing red herrings of this nature but to encourage the young men of India to achieve new standards on the field of play. Many of them followed his advice. Greig had taken over the conference from the manager Ken Barrington who had shown signs of becoming rattled by some of the more direct questions.

In the Fourth Test Foster bowled magnificently, taking twelve wickets in the match. Thanks to Graeme Fowler and Mike Gatting who both made double centuries – the first time two England batsmen had scored double centuries in the same innings in the same Test match – England built up a first-innings lead of 380 and went on to win by nine wickets.

In the final Test in Kanpur England held on for the draw which gave them victory in the series by two matches to one and was a pretty considerable achievement.

After England's annihilation at the hands of the West Indies the immediate future looked bleak, but in India several of the newer players had shown that they were well worth their chance. Tim Robinson, the Nottinghamshire opener, was one of them and Fowler, although by now assured of his place, confirmed most good impressions. At last Mike Gatting, who had been given every opportunity at this level without grasping any of them, made good with a century and a double century and for the first time for a while England had not been short of runs. But with Graham Gooch available from May 1985 the two openers may be hard pressed to keep their places. Paul Downton had had another useful series with the bat although not such a successful one with the wicketkeeping gloves. While the two spinners Phil Edmonds and Pat Pocock had done a good deal of the bowling, Foster had won the Fourth Test and Norman Cowans had taken some important wickets but Ellison's figures did him less than justice. Unfortunately injury had caused Paul Allott to go home early and his place had been taken by Jonathan Agnew, who still has great problems with his control. By all accounts Gower and Gatting, who was his aggressive vice-captain, ran a most happy side with a wonderful team spirit. On leaving India there were those who were prepared to say that one of the reasons for the excellent spirit was the absence of Botham. Much was written in the English press about this and I even heard that Botham himself had been prompted to ring up the manager, Tony Brown (who is also the secretary of Somerset) and ask what was going on. It was Brown's first experience of managership and he could hardly have been given a worse start with the two assassinations in India, but he came through it with his reputation greatly enhanced and he was by no means the least of the reasons why this was such a happy England party. As far as Botham is concerned, the side's success in India means that when he does return to England colours it will be on Gower and Gatting's terms and not on his own. The only partial sadness in India was Gower's own inability to score runs and this was another illustration of the difficulty modern captains face in fulfilling the demanding role of captaincy without allowing it to affect their form as players. But when England left India its cricket seemed healthier than it had for some time.

The other series which was taking place at this time was the return between Pakistan and New Zealand in New Zealand. This time, the New Zealanders with Geoff Howarth back in charge and Richard Hadlee in the side – neither had gone to Pakistan – made short shrift of Pakistan's batting and New Zealand gained revenge for their defeat in Pakistan. It was yet another series which saw politics erupt in the Pakistan camp. Javed Miandad had returned to the captaincy, but it was not long, I heard, before some of the side were ganging up against him. Imran Khan once told me that Javed had the outlook of a 'street-fighter' and I daresay his passions rather than his common sense take over when he is in charge. I doubt this is the best way to captain any side, let alone Pakistan where almost everyone else's passions are always about to take over. Towards the end of the tour Pakistan were playing in Wellington under the captaincy of Zaheer Abbas, who has never been the most sympathetic handler of spin bowlers. Abdul Qadir, the leg-spinner whose bouts with the authorities have become more frequent and more tiresome, objected to his treatment and at one stage left the field in protest. Apparently events were relayed by telephone to the President of the Board of Control for Cricket in Pakistan, General Safdar Butt, who had no hesitation in recommending that the culprit be sent home.

This then was the frenetic international scene around the cricketing world in these few months, but the greatest dramas of all which I have deliberately left until now, had taken place in Brisbane in November. Before Australia and the West Indies had begun their series, Kim Hughes had been appointed as captain of Australia and he was the only choice. Twelve months before he had kept the job fighting off a spirited challenge by Rod Marsh after Greg Chappell's retirement. He had since taken Australia to the West Indies where these days it is no disgrace to lose. He had captained the side on a short tour to India for a series of one-day matches where he had presided over a happy side which had won at the same time as developing a fine team spirit. Hughes himself seemed more relaxed yet more determined than ever. He knew now without fear of contradiction that it was his own ship.

It was unfortunate that he should have developed a bad habit of talking too freely to the press and indeed to anyone who would listen. His every utterance was full of optimism and always received great publicity and one might have been forgiven for thinking that Australia were halfway towards beating the West Indies. As a captain, Hughes had always allowed himself to become too easily dispirited and if he had not made runs himself this was usually reflected by his demeanour in the field. More than most he needed the confidence of his own success. Against the West Indies in the Caribbean he had gone for five Test Matches without getting out of the thirties. There was therefore a fair amount of pressure on him before a ball had been bowled by the West Indians in Australia.

In the First Test in Perth the West Indians lost five first-innings wickets for 104 before recovering to 416 all out. Hughes's captaincy was not good and when Gomes and Dujon, both of whom made centuries, were batting so well, Hughes seemed to become devoid of ideas and to lose control. He had always been a captain who has waited for something to happen and then reacted subjectively rather than one who tried to make things happen. He does not have an incisive cricket brain and I always felt that he was a captain who allowed himself to be overtaken by events. Had he not been seen by the Australian Cricket Board at the time of the uneasy peace treaty with World Series Cricket as their talisman in the struggle against WSC, I doubt he would have held on to the job for so long, for his record was not good. At that time Greg Chappell was the natural captain for Australia but if ever he was unable to play or to go on tour, Hughes was always the next choice. When Marsh lost his battle to take over from Hughes at the start of the 1983/84 season, his ability to do the job may well have come second to other considerations. The Australian Cricket Board made the decision. Marsh had always been a pillar of WSC (as I have shown in the opening chapters) and would not have been thought likely to project the traditional image of an Australian Test captain even if he did have the support of Mr Fred Bennett, the chairman of the Board.

In 1984/85 Hughes's first hostage to fortune was his public promise not to hook, the shot which had frequently landed him in trouble in the Caribbean and had got him out in the second innings of Western Australia's game with the West Indies. On the third morning of the First Test in Perth Australia were 36/3 with Hughes and Border at the crease. Four runs had been scored when Hughes was out, well caught by Marshall running to his left at fine leg off a wild hook he had played at Holding and it was not long before Australia had been bowled out for 76. They followed on and did not fare significantly better the second time round, losing by an innings and 112 runs. Hughes was already in trouble. The action now moved on to Brisbane and the Australian selectors, Laurie Sawle, the chairman who comes from Western Australia, Greg Chappell from Queensland and Rick

McCosker of New South Wales brought the two spinners, Bennett and Holland (who had just bowled New South Wales to victory over the West Indies) into the squad for the Second Test match. Chappell was the senior selector present at the match and although events at Brisbane are still a little bit 'according to the last person you spoke to', a distillation has produced an account which is not too far off course.

Whether by accident or design, Chappell was on his way to becoming the most powerful figure in Australian cricket. It was Chappell, presumably because he was the senior selector in Brisbane, who attended the dinner the Australians held on the evening before the match. In Australia it is unusual for a selector to be present on these occasions. By all accounts, Chappell had some strong words to say to the players, especially those involved in the defeats in the first two Test Matches. It was a speech which I would have thought could only have undermined Hughes's authority within the side. Some time in the build up to the Second Test, Chappell also had a conversation with Hughes himself which included more plain speaking and his future as Australia's captain was on the agenda, together with his prospects for holding on to the job. One school of thought had it that Chappell was anxious to end Hughes's term of office for, like his brother Ian, Greg had never been one of Hughes's most fervent admirers. He well knew that the Australian Cricket Board, who had stood squarely by Hughes, would not be prepared to vote him out of office. To have done so would have made a mockery of their decision to give him the job in front of Marsh a year earlier. Hughes had, therefore, to be persuaded to resign. Chappell might have found a supporter for his views in the chairman of the ACB, Mr Fred Bennett, who had voted for Marsh a year earlier, but it is not certain that Mr Bennett knew what was going on. The weekend at the new Brisbane Sheraton, which is a marvellously comfortable hotel, was full of hushed and whispered conversations in the coffee shop and doubtless too, behind closed doors in the rooms upstairs. I got the impression that there may have been people involved who did not want it to become public knowledge.

Australia lost in four days, as had always seemed inevitable, and after the match the press assembled in the players' dining room for the usual post-match captains' press conferences. Hughes answered questions about the contest and then just when it seemed that he had finished he brought out a piece of paper and announced that he had a statement he wished to read out. He now became emotional, which was hardly surprising considering he was about to read out his own resignation from the job he coveted above all others. Halfway through it all became too much for him and he handed the paper to the team manager, Bob Merriman, so that he could finish reading it. It transpired that two of the people who knew of the resignation before it was made – and apparently had known for most of the day for Hughes had made up his mind in the morning – were Greg Chappell and Merriman, who as the Australian summer wore on became an increasingly enigmatic figure. Chappell and Merriman may have been the only two to have known but unfortunately it seems Fred Bennett was not informed of Hughes's intention to resign until five minutes before Hughes began to read his statement. If Bennett had known he would surely have done all he could to persuade Hughes to change his mind, although there are those who say he was told. No one who had the interests of Australian cricket at heart could have wanted to change captains in mid-series. On past tours of Australia I have always had the impression that Merriman was a great supporter of Hughes. I do not know what pressure, if any, was put on Hughes during the day to make him change his mind. One day, I daresay, the full facts will be known and there are any number of grey areas to clear up. I wonder if any two accounts will ever tally in all the details. One thing is sure: Hughes was soon bitterly to regret his decision to resign, which suggests that he might have been swayed. As it was, he probably imagined daggers at his back when they were not that close. For all that, it was impossible not to feel desperately sorry for him.

It is now necessary to try and put some flesh on the bare bones of Bob Merriman. He had for some time been an Arbitration Commissioner and while doing that job he had for a few seasons been the disciplinary officer for the ACB. As such, he had to sit in judgment on various members of the Australian side reported by the umpires who had then appealed when they felt that the penalty imposed on the players concerned by the players' own disciplinary committee had not been severe enough. Lillee was one who had come up in front of him on more than one occasion. Merriman probably saw himself more as a conciliator than a judge, for that was what he was in real life, and his penalties were not known for their severity. In fact, there were times when they were so light that they could hardly be said to uphold the rule of authority. Then, sometime in 1984, the ACB decided they wanted a permanent manager who would look after the Australian side at home and away for the next eighteen months. Merriman took leave of absence from the Arbitration Commission for eighteen months and was given the job. He was now touching fifty and he had in his time been quite a decent District cricketer with Geelong, but he had had no first-class experience.

It was not an altogether happy time for him at first. While the Australians had been in the West Indies earlier in 1984, they had not been noted for their tactful behaviour on the field or off it. Lawson in particular had overstepped the mark and a battle had developed between Lawson and Haynes, normally the mildest and most disarming of men, so much so that it is natural to feel that anyone who picks a row with him must himself be at fault. When Lawson throws a tantrum it is, too, almost invariably irritating, childish and offensive. In Brisbane, Australia lost, but the West Indies lost two wickets while scoring the 23 runs they needed for victory in their second innings. Haynes and Lawson were hardly enjoying each other's company and it looked more than once as if they were having words. The West Indies had almost won when Haynes was bowled by Lawson, who bounced down the pitch making no secret of his feelings and more words were exchanged. As he started to leave the field, Haynes spun round and gave Lawson a powerful and obvious V-sign which earned him a severe rebuke from Clive Lloyd, who said that if any of his side did that again they would be sent home. The West Indies management made an official complaint about Lawson's behaviour but as far as I know nothing was done about it.

It was clear that there was plenty of feeling between the two sides and it erupted again during the Third Test in Adelaide. When Lawson was out, he did not appear to be over-anxious to depart. Richards at first slip and Dujon behind the stumps had something to say on the matter and Wessels walked down from the non-striker's end and had his two bob's worth. Wessels did not seem to be a favourite with the West Indians and it is likely that his South African origins were the reason. The feeling, by the way, was mutual. The West Indians may have decided that they would accept 'sledging' from, say, Englishmen and Australians, but not from South Africans. During this match Greg Chappell saw Lloyd and Richards in an attempt to defuse the situation.

Whatever hostilities were simmering during the Fourth Test in Melbourne were kept below the surface until the fourth day. Australia had saved the follow-on with their last pair together and the West Indies began their second innings 183 runs ahead. Lawson bowled the first over to Gordon Greenidge, who shuffled across his stumps and survived a confident lbw appeal – Steve Randall, the first Tasmanian to stand in a Test Match, was the umpire and he had an excellent first Test. Lawson was most unhappy with the decision and after registering all sorts of profound disbelief halfway down the pitch, he tore off his sleeveless sweater, stalked past the umpire and gave it to Border at mid-off. Border carried the sweater the twenty yards or so to the stumps and gave it to the umpire. At the end of the over Randall offered Lawson his hat and sweater but Lawson brushed rudely past him and walked abruptly down to fine leg. Randall took the garments over to Border, had a short conversation with him and Border took them all the way down to his fast bowler at fine leg. I do not remember seeing a bowler humiliate an umpire as Lawson did then. Lillee may have gone through his tantrums but I never saw him try to make a fool of an umpire like this. In his next over Lawson again hit Greenidge on the pads and this time won the decision. As Greenidge set off to the pavilion, Lawson felt it necessary to send him away with gestures and a torrent of abuse, so much so that in turn Greenidge himself decided to pay a visit to the Australian dressing room during the lunch interval after receiving permission from Border, to tell Lawson a few home truths. At one point Lawson is supposed to have asked Greenidge what he had done wrong. Greenidge replied, 'So, you've got amnesia too,' or words along those lines.

Wes Hall, the West Indies manager, made an official complaint to the ACB about Lawson's behaviour, which will have been seen at first hand by several members of the Board who were on the ground. It was time for the wheels of the disciplinary process to go round once again. But nothing happened, for public consumption at any rate, until we had all foregathered in Sydney for the Fifth Test. Then, Merriman announced one afternoon before the match began that two issues had been considered and action had been taken. Merriman had hung on to his disciplinary powers in spite of his appointment as team manager. The first issue, he said, was the incident between Lawson and Greenidge when Greenidge was out, and the second was Lawson's overall behaviour and attitude. On the first count no action would be taken, for the players had got together and talked it out. As far as the second was concerned, Merriman had decided to fine Lawson two thousand dollars, five hundred of which were payable immediately while the payment of the remaining fifteen hundred was suspended until March 1986 – which in effect meant that Lawson had been placed under a good conduct bond for fifteen months. It was a profound relief that those in authority had at last been prepared to take action to curb Lawson although it seemed a crazy system of justice whereby the team manager was forced to sit in judgment on his own players. It could hardly have led to warmth and understanding in the dressing room. It may well have been that Merriman was told by the ACB that he had to take action even though the foreseeable result was that he was no longer held in universal admiration by the Australian side.

In fact, Merriman's decision, whether it was his own or forced upon him, caused considerable trouble which built up during the Test Match in Sydney. On the second day it took a good deal of hard talking to persuade Border, who had wholeheartedly taken up Lawson's cause, not to boycott the remainder of the match. The team was split down the middle over the issue and while some players agreed with Border and Lawson, there were others whose only concern was to get on with the job of playing cricket. It was hardly edifying, either, to see Australia's captain defend such reprehensible and unforgivable behaviour as Lawson's in Melbourne. The issue festered on for some time and Greg Chappell, who was having a holiday, came to Sydney to talk to the players and to remind them of their duty.

At an executive meeting of the ACB in Hobart which was attended by Merriman and Border the time of Lawson's good conduct bond was reduced from fifteen to three months, although the findings of the meeting were, it was thought at the time, going to be confidential. Border himself announced in Sydney soon afterwards that the entire Australian team would share the fine which he still felt to be unfair. He also said he wanted the money given to the Ethiopian Relief Fund and not the ACB. Some of the team were not happy about sharing the fine and one player at least made it clear in private that he would have nothing to do with it. In the end the $500 was deducted from a future match fee which was paid to Lawson.

Although Border had only been in the job for three Test matches he was prepared to take on his bosses in a head-on clash and it appears that in revealing the details of the meeting in Hobart he had gone directly against the wishes of the meeting. Border is a determined cricketer and a gritty batsman who always sells his wicket dearly. He is also an obstinate man of fixed views and on the evidence of three Tests against the West Indies a limited captain who does not have any real flair for the job. He was a consensus choice after Hughes's resignation and by his subsequent actions he will not have endeared himself to his employers. When the Board had to decide on Hughes's successor,

David Hookes of South Australia will have had his supporters for he is probably the best of the state captains in Australia and I felt he was the man for the job. In realistic terms, therefore, these were the only two candidates, but Hookes has been the sort of character all through his career who could not help making enemies as well as friends. He was one of the few remaining members of World Series Cricket still playing and he had always modelled himself on Ian Chappell and aligned himself with WSC's leading protagonists. Although this should now have been forgotten it may have counted against him, although I do not think his candidature reached the stage where this became a consideration. For all Ian Chappell's support I am not sure that Hookes was a favourite of Greg Chappell's, which in these circumstances was what mattered. Since he has been captain of South Australia Hookes has been lucky to have had Australia's most knowledgeable cricketer, John Inverarity, playing under him. Before moving to Adelaide, Inverarity had been a most successful captain of Western Australia and now his influence had had a great effect upon Hookes. It is a measure of Hookes's achievements that the young players in the South Australian side are developing so well in the atmosphere he has created.

Hookes's biggest problem has been his own inconsistent form with the bat. He is an exciting left-hander who has played some remarkable innings for South Australia and he has at times been prepared as a captain to take a gamble which is no bad thing. He toured the West Indies with Hughes's side in 1984, but on his return he was not included in the list of sixteen players put under contract by the ACB. The selectors had probably grown wary of him and felt that he had had his chance and that it was time to turn to someone younger. During his career too, he might easily have alienated Greg Chappell and Rick McCosker, both contemporaries. In the final analysis, the selectors will have picked their side for the Third Test Match in Adelaide, which will *not* have included Hookes and the names will then have gone in front of the full Board for the captain to be chosen. With Border the only candidate in the side, the decision will not have taken long. I could not help wondering how Rod Marsh would have been feeling, for if he had had any idea that this situation might arise he would not have retired when he did.

Border's willingness to fight the Board so soon after his appointment will not have helped his popularity with the powers that be, but he had the luck to win the Fifth Test Match and also one of the three finals for the Benson & Hedges World Series Cup and this will have helped consolidate his position. With Hookes not in the side, although I felt the selectors were wrong not to pick him for the one-day tournament, there was no alternative to Border to captain the side in England in 1985. Border was in more trouble early in the New Year for there was another outbreak of resentment during the Fifth Test. In the West Indies first innings the Australians thought that Viv Richards had been caught by Wood at forward short leg off bat and pad. Umpire Isherwood standing in his first Test Match thought differently. Wicketkeeper Rixon's violent appeal took him some way down the wicket towards the umpire and after the appeal had been turned down he and Richards began a conversation. Border now came running in from cover on what he later described as a peace mission, but when he arrived he at once became involved. At the end of the day's play all three players were reported by the umpires. The cockeyed system of justice now ordained that the two Australian players would be tried by three of their colleagues, Wood, Wessels and Hilditch, who met the next morning before the start of play. It was no big surprise when they came to the conclusion that the exchanges had been started by Richards and that their captain and their wicketkeeper had no charge to answer. The umpires did not appeal, which made one wonder why they bothered to report them in the first place. Wes Hall, meanwhile, had denied the charges against Richards, saying that the player had told him the truth and indeed Richards's account was backed up in detail by those who tuned their radio receivers into the wave length of the television microphone at the bottom of the stumps. From that evidence Richards could only have been replying to something which had been said to him when he suggested that Rixon need only to name the place and they would settle it all afterwards. Richards claimed he was called a cheat. One of Border's legitimate protests was, why should disciplinary procedures be applied to one side and not the other? Perhaps the biggest surprise of all was that after Border's criticisms of the ACB, the chairman and the other officers involved decided to take no public action so that the Board was seen to be in control of its own house. One feels that they may have created a precedent they may come to regret.

Relations were never easy all season between the Australians and the West Indians. But Merriman's fining of Lawson had had one spectacular result in that it had quietened down his behaviour to a remarkable extent in the second half of the season. So we all now know that he can control himself when he wants to, which will make any excesses in the future, when the good behaviour bond has expired, even more unforgivable. He has set a precedent for himself. By the time the West Indies had won the World Series Cup, those who had pursued the game through the length and breadth of Australia for the last four months were perhaps not looking forward as much as they might have done to the World Championship of Cricket. But with all seven Test playing countries involved it at least meant some new faces, which was a little like seeing the cavalry come over the horizon. Before the competition began with the match between Australia and England at the Melbourne Cricket Ground, with the floodlights switched on for the first time, I managed to pinch three delicious days at Hamilton Island, Australia's newest and most plush Holiday Resort in the Whitsunday Islands on the Great Barrier Reef.

17
Further Adventures

In spite of a considerable build up, the World Championship of Cricket never really caught the imagination of the Australian public. The Victorian Cricket Association, whose idea it was, had not, in their determination to ensure that it came off, taken into account the full implications of starting another one-day competition five days after the eighteen matches for the Benson & Hedges World Series Cup had finished. They were perhaps blinded by their desire to see floodlights at the Melbourne Cricket Ground and the 150th anniversary celebrations for the founding of the State of Victoria provided them with a wonderful chance. Realizing the importance of the occasion, the Victorian Labour Government of John Cain made an important contribution to the cost which would not otherwise have been forthcoming. Although the erection of the lights caused fierce union battles while they were being put up, six huge, ghostly, white floodlight pylons appeared and brought a new dimension to the MCG.

Far from causing any great aesthetic harm to a ground which is in essence a vast football stadium, they seemed to give it a more satisfying finish. At the Sydney Cricket Ground the six black pylons still look like an unwarranted intrusion and even with the big modern stands strike a visual note which is still harsh and discordant.

While the VCA understood the importance of floodlights to the MCG, they were unlucky in that the World Championship of Cricket turned out to be a promoter's nightmare, with India and Pakistan fighting their way through to the final which restricted the gate to 35,000 on that occasion. The VCA were unable to recoup as much of the cost of the lights from the competition as they would have liked. But the lights are bound to increase the attraction of the ground to public and promoters alike and they will soon pay for themselves. The opening match of the competition had been carefully planned and was played between the two old enemies, England and Australia, and more than 82,000 came to the MCG probably as much to see the lights switched on for the first time as to watch the cricket. As it happened England, who had just finished a demanding and successful tour of India, made a mess of it after twice reaching positions which might have led to victory and were conclusively beaten by seven wickets, which from Australia's point of view was a perfect start to the competition.

While staying on Hamilton Island for the few days between the two competitions, I ran into Alan Johnson and Alan Morris, who make the cricket commercials in Australia. They told me that contests between England and Australia are still the only ones which need no advertising. Even allowing for the new lights, the number of spectators at this first match gave solid backing to their argument. The next largest gate, which was for the final, produced almost 50,000 fewer spectators. Interest in the competition waned partly because Australia made no sort of showing but mainly because the public had had enough one-day international cricket to last it for one season. The prices for ground entrance and for the various stands which are set by PBL Marketing, had risen to the level where members of the public, no matter how keen, had to ration their appearances at these contests for simple economic reasons. PBL, through its managing director Lynton Taylor, was later to argue vehemently against the objection that there was too much one-day international cricket – and I could not help feeling that Taylor is either a sado-masochist or crucially out of touch with the reality of the situation. There is an important financial need for one-day cricket in Australia, but at the moment those in authority seem to have got it out of proportion. A blend of one-day and Test cricket is acceptable for everyone, but thirty-one limited-over internationals in a row is altogether to much of a good thing.

After being defeated at home by England, India, who had of course beaten the West Indies in the final of the World Cup at Lord's in 1983, now proceeded to carry all before them in Australia although the privilege of knocking the West Indies out of the competition was left to Pakistan – a frustratingly unpredictable side. India were capably led by Gavaskar, had the two spinners, Sivaramakrishnan and Shastri, four good seam bowlers (all of whom batted well enough to count as all-rounders) and in 20-year-old Mohammed Azharuddin the best young batsman in the world. In the series against England he had become the first batsman ever to score a hundred in each of his first three Test Matches. India played five matches in Australia and bowled out their opponents inside the fifty overs on four occasions; indeed, took nine Pakistan wickets on the fifth which was the final. Only New Zealand, who reached 206, managed to score more than 200 against them and the immediate future of Indian cricket is extremely bright, which must be good for the game.

Pakistan were captained with glorious unpredictability by Javed Miandad, who still does not appear to have the full backing of his players as happened when he first captained Pakistan in Australia in 1981/82. They looked a better side than they had done in Australia the year before and one of the reasons for this was that the stress fracture to Imran's left shin had now mended. He gave the attack a new impetus although at thirty-two he will almost certainly never again be as fast as he was before the injury. Pakistan have also found an exciting newcomer in Wasim Akram, who bowls left arm over the wicket at fast medium and destroyed the Australian innings when he took 5/21 in eight overs. They have another outstanding young player in Rameez Raja, the younger brother of Wasim Raja, who played a brilliant innings of sixty to help Pakistan beat the West Indies in the semi-final. He has marvellous footwork which enabled him to hook Marshall and even Garner with impunity. He is a player to watch, while Mohsin and Mudassar showed that as an opening pair they are almost the equal of Greenidge and Haynes.

After a hard tour of India the England players came to Australia anxious to relax rather than to fight hard in the middle, which was understandable if unfortunate. They never really knuckled down to the job in hand which I felt was mildly insulting to their hosts, although when they lost to India in Sydney their fielding was the best I can remember from an England side. They lost all three of their preliminary matches and so failed to qualify for the semi-finals and rather more surprisingly Australia became another casualty. After beating England they lost to both Pakistan and India, which was a blow for the promoters although both matches were played in front of surprisingly small crowds at the MCG. In the first semi-final the West Indies, who had always seemed the likely winners, batted like men in a dream against Pakistan. They had played only one match in more than two weeks and obviously had difficulty in motivating themselves for one last effort. The result was that Clive Lloyd's last international appearance was as a losing semi-finalist, which was not the way the script had been written. Victory over Sri Lanka, who had had the stuffing knocked out of them in the Benson & Hedges World Series Cup, had taken New Zealand into the semi-final where they were no match for India.

It was an excellent advertisement for the game of cricket that the competition should have thrown up two such unlikely finalists. The crowd at the final was very much a cricket-loving and not a beer-swilling audience. On the day, as had seemed likely, India were much too good for Pakistan. I remember, as I left the MCG that night and walked back through the Fitzroy Gardens for the last time that season, feeling profoundly relieved that it was all over. Most of us in the media had had to endure all thirty-one successive limited-over matches while the public at large could at least pick and choose as they wanted. And there was always the television. It had been a season with too few upsets; moments of light relief had been as rare as close results and so it was an especially welcome bonus when Lynton Taylor, the afore-mentioned boss of PBL Marketing, unleashed upon us all a few moments of pure farce when it was over. Taylor was very much to the forefront in the heady days of 1977 when World Series Cricket was founded and Kerry Packer took on the game's Establishment. Out-wardly at any rate, he was in his boss's shadow, but I am sure that behind the scenes he played an important role. Since those days he has consistently behaved as if he is still bitter at the way in which WSC was opposed by those who ran the traditional game. He has seldom wasted a chance of forecasting the eventual eclipse of Test cricket by the limited-over game and of expressing sentiments which would hardly have pleased his erstwhile opponents.

He had been conspicuously absent from the cricket played during the 1984/85 Australian season and when I shook him by the hand in the press room during the final in Melbourne, it was the first time I had set eyes on him in five months. In his rather distant manner he expressed surprise that I was still in Australia as England had been knocked out. As we were watching the final of the competition this surprised me and I suggested that if he had been a reader of *The Australian* he would know that I wrote a daily column in the paper. Looking at the wall, he assured me that he was a reader of *The Australian* and that he was unaware that I wrote for the paper. In this same week, which began on the Sunday with the final, Taylor gave interviews to various newspapers in which he complained strongly that the criticisms of the Australian season had come from jealous English administrators and had been fanned by the English press. He went on to say that the Poms could not tolerate the fact that the Australian' Cricket Board had been able to do a deal with Packer when their own administrators had failed. He added that the Australian season was now much more successful than the English season and that the centre of cricket had moved from England to Australia. Also he did not rule out the possibility of an increase in the amount of one-day cricket in Australia. I waited anxiously for the chairman of the Australian Cricket Board, Fred Bennett, to enter a loud protest that it was the Board and not Mr Taylor who arranged the season's programme. As nothing was forthcoming I could only wonder at the power of Mr Taylor. At all events, I wrote him an open letter in *The Australian* couched in reasonably severe terms and I daresay that the next time he sees me in an Australian press box he will know why I am there even if the Englishmen are not playing.

The World Championship of Cricket final was not quite the end. In a wonderful game of cricket, New South Wales beat Queensland by one wicket in the final of the Sheffield Shield competition. It was undoubtedly the best game of the season, but received no television coverage and PBL Marketing never explained why this should have been so; at least if they did I never heard the explanation. There should have been questions in Parliament. Queensland, who have been trying since 1926, have still to win a Sheffield Shield title. The next morning the Australian selectors announced the names of the seventeen players to tour England in the Australian winter. Rumour had it that Kim Hughes had been assured of a place but his name was not on the list. There may have been a late change of mind or maybe Greg Chappell, a strong opponent of Hughes, had persuaded Rick McCosker to side with him against chairman Lawrie Sawle, who is from Western Australia, and that in return he told McCosker he could be sure of Chappell's support for certain of the New South Wales players. The day after the side was announced Border took a thirteen-man party to Sharjah in the United Arab Emirates to play India, Pakistan and England for the Asian Cup. Hughes was in that party and at the time of writing it remains to be seen if he decides on his return home that he has had enough. I would not blame him if he had, for I wonder if the game of cricket has ever treated a player more shabbily or more shamefully than Kimberley John Hughes. It would be nice to think those responsible will one day have to answer for their actions.

While so much of the cricket and its politics was less than heroic, the tour had its moments of compensation off the field. From my own point of view, one of the most amusing moments of the season happened at the MCG on Boxing Day. I had spent a typically thirsty Christmas evening at a delightful party in Brighton and I was none too bright when I woke up the following morning, which was the fourth day of the Fourth Test Match. After shaving by numbers, I made good use of the Jacuzzi in my suite at Irvin Rockman's splendid Regency Hotel and then grabbed the first pair of trousers I could lay my hands on and in due time stumbled through the Fitzroy Gardens past Captain Cook's cottage in time for an eleven o'clock start. After about an hour's play I set off for the Long Room in the Pavilion to collect my supply of beef sandwiches for lunch. At the far end of the Long Room bar, Dorothy and her colleagues have been dispensing these delicious sandwiches for years and they are the best at any cricket ground in the world. She always makes three for me using the rarest beef she can find and brown bread and butter and I nip in early to collect them.

As always, I showed my pass to the steward at the entrance to the pavilion and walked on past the library and the Melbourne Cricket Club committee rooms to the entrance of the Long Room. I flashed my pass again to the attendant there and walked on, but a young lady wearing a badge of office now stepped out from my right and told me most charmingly that denim jeans were not allowed in the Long Room. I looked quickly down at my trousers. I did not have a clue which pair I was wearing, such were the circumstances of my health when I got up that morning. Of course, they were jeans and I apologized profusely and beat a hasty retreat. In the press box I repeated the story to Alan Shiell, who writes for the *Adelaide Advertiser*, and we had a good laugh. Then, just before lunch by the commentary boxes, I bumped into Tom Prior who once wrote the cricket for the *Melbourne Sun* and is now their chief reporter and leading columnist and an old friend of mine. Alan Shiell had told him the story and he wanted to use it for his column the next day. I made him promise not to send up the MCG, for they were quite right to kick me out and I would never have tried to go into the Lord's pavilion in a pair of jeans. Tom insisted his photographer had a go at me and the next morning I found my jeans had been immortalized by his splendid pen. It was all in high good humour. The next day the monster electronic scoreboard at the MCG, which is controlled by a spectacular blonde called Anna, referred to me once or twice when the board was listing the names of the commentary team for Radio 3AW, as 'Blue Jeans Blofeld'. It was all good fun except possibly for poor old Dorothy, who was left with three delicious sandwiches.

The most unlikely cricket match I came across was played almost in the shadow of Ayer's Rock in the Northern Territory. Two days after the final in Melbourne Ian Meckiff, whose career was ended when he was no-balled for throwing by umpire Col Eagar in the First Test between Australia and South Africa in Brisbane in 1962/63, and I flew by small aeroplane from Melbourne to the old mining town of Broken Hill by way of Mildura, which in one of its clubs proudly possesses the longest bar in the world. In Broken Hill, which like all other mining towns I have ever been to has an atmosphere of the wild West with its wide streets and mass of pubs, Ian and I spoke at a sportsman's night at the Broken Hill Football Club and then flew off at half past eight the next morning in another small aeroplane to Adelaide. There, we joined about forty others who were being taken up to Ayer's Rock by Sheraton Hotels. They had arranged a cricket match at the Yulara Oval for the following day. Just about the first person I came across was Colin Cowdrey, who nowadays works for Barclays Bank and was captaining one of the sides. He was surrounded by other influential members of the Bank who were going up to Yulara to cast an eye over their investment there, which has worked out at about thirty million dollars. During the last two years a remarkable resort has been built in the middle of the desert about twelve miles from the Rock. At present it consists principally of two hotels, the largest of which is the newly opened Ayer's Rock Sheraton. Visually, it is a stunning building. All the rooms, with their terraced balconies just three floors high, open on to a large swimming pool and garden like a magical oasis, though at the back, the desert creeps up to the very foot of the building. The main complex is spacious and airy and it soon found its way into my personal list of hotels which are to be revisited as soon as possible.

Our flight from Adelaide to Alice Springs, by kind permission of TAA, was faultless but we then had to embark in an air-conditioned bus for the drive to the Rock. The aeroplane, which takes less than an hour, was booked out, so for five-and-a-half hours I sat in the back of this bus next door to the loo while we drove down just about the straightest road in the world with a mixture of desert and undergrowth and nothing stretching away for ever on either side. This drive, more than any aeroplane journey I have ever made – including the flight from Perth across the Nullarbor Plain – illustrated perfectly the vast nothingness of the continent of Australia. We made three pit stops along the way for further intakes of beer and when we arrived at the hotel we were either tired or pissed, according to taste. No sooner had we set foot on the ground than we were shepherded on a ten-minute walk to a hillock where cocktails were served and we watched the sun go down on the Rock, which changed in a second from its intriguing red brick colour to the oblivion of deep shadow. The Rock could hardly have got off to a more impressive start.

I was so inspired that I arranged a call at a quarter to six the next morning and with former Australian wicketkeeper Kevin Wright decided to attempt the climb. After some excellent coffee we went aboard another bus which was already full of American tourists all strung around with cameras and looking like so many Father Christmases and set to conquer 'That Godamned Rock'. I was decidedly apprehensive by the time we had arrived at the foot of the largest monolith in the world for it looked impossibly steep and the track that we would be expected to climb was at times little short of vertical. I suppose there was a time when I would have relished the challenge. As it was I looked around hoping that I might find someone who was feeling his 'hamstring' and felt the climb would be unwise. I had no such luck and so, with Kevin alongside, off I set. The walk to the top was about sixteen hundred metres and the first part of the climb, which I was assured was the worst, stretched away for a third of that distance. I must have climbed about a hundred yards and was panting away, hanging on to a chain which must have been put there for dwarves for it came up to my knees and meant that I was climbing in a stooping position. My calf and thigh muscles began to scream and it suddenly occurred to me that I had come to Ayer's Rock for two days to enjoy myself. So, with a mild attack of cowardice coming on, I beat a pretty hasty retreat. I was pleased that when Kevin had climbed about twice as far, he came to the same conclusion. I realized what a good decision I had made when on returning to ground level I noticed a series of plaques in the foot of the rock. They had been put there in memory of those intrepid souls who had put their cues in the rack for the last time while making the climb. For all that, I was put to shame by the assortment of middle-aged Americans of both sexes – and some were older than that – who scaled the heights like a bunch of mountain goats. When I got back to the hotel I found a cap in the shop which said on the front 'I tried to climb Ayer's Rock'. I bought it and wore it for the rest of the day.

The cricket, which began at half past nine, was genial and uncompetitive and when I reach the Oval, which was green and in excellent condition, I found that Ian Meckiff (the Count) had bowled his three overs under the eagle eye of Col. Egar umpiring at square leg and had been given a clean bill of health. No sooner had I taken over the ground commentary from Alan McGilvray than Egar gave Colin Cowdrey out lbw to a deliberate chuck by the Sheraton sales director in Australasia, Leon Larkin, who had masterminded the two days. Larkin finished with career best figures of 1/35 in three overs. We had a two-hour break for lunch, which was barely time to negotiate a superb mixed grill, and in the afternoon Rod Marsh's side failed to reach a target of 299. There was an ugly incident when a former chairman of the Australian Cricket Board, Phil Ridings, while umpiring at square leg, fielded the ball, threw it back to the wicketkeeper and then gave the batsman run out. That evening we had a big dinner round the pool with a myriad of speeches and enough noise to keep the dingoes awake and it was a quarter past two before I boarded an aeroplane at the neighbouring airport which decanted me in Perth before dawn had broken.

Another improbable cricket event occurred when on the last day of my visit to Keith Williams's spectacular new holiday resort at Hamilton Island, I was asked to don pads, gloves and bat with only bathing pants underneath and to pat back gentle full tosses to the island's new managing director, David Crompton. Richard Magnus, who supervises everything from dry martinis to hiring catamarans, fielded at silly mid off with his camera. I daresay these photographs were outdated when David Gower, Allan Lamb and one or two other England players visited the island after they had been knocked out of the World Championship of Cricket.

Keith Williams has leased the island for ninety-nine years from the Queensland Government and is in the process of spending more than two hundred and fifty million dollars to make it into the most perfect holiday resort in the Pacific. Though only about 400 out of an eventual 2000 bedrooms were ready for occupation and it was the monsoon season, it was still busy enough. Two years ago the island was an uninhabited swamp when Williams, whose last venture was to construct Seaworld on Queensland's Gold Coast, had begun to develop it. He has only been allowed to touch a quarter of it, but already he and Ansett Airlines have in partnership laid down a 6000-foot runway which will take anything up to short-bodied jumbos and there are direct flights from the main Australian cities. The main complex, built delightfully in Hawaiian style, is finished; restaurants are springing up all over the place, the marina is in full operation, speedboats abound and all the amenities like tennis and squash courts are in action. A conference centre is going up and so also are two of the four high-rise apartment blocks. It has all been most thoroughly landscaped and blends in beautifully with the natural scenery. Helicopters buzz everywhere taking guests to pontoons moored in the sea and also the thirty-odd kilometres out to the Great Barrier Reef itself. There is a small mountain which it takes an hour-and-a-half to climb and if the climber is too tired to make the return journey, he waves a flag and a helicopter will bring him back.

There will soon be a luxurious floating hotel which will take guests out to the Reef for four days at a time and in the northern part of the island, plots of land have been sold to people who want to build their own houses – one of these has been bought by George Harrison. The second stage of the development will see the rounded point at the north end turned into a Riviera-style resort with rows of terraced houses, a plethora of restaurants and maybe a casino. The pool in the main complex by Catseye Beech is said to be the biggest freshwater pool in the southern hemisphere and it has an island in the middle where a bar dispenses every known form of liquid luxury. There is a pool by the main restaurant, the Dolphin Room, which houses three dolphins. It is all the most superbly comfortable upmarket desert island anyone has ever invented. I don't know what Robinson Crusoe would make of it, but he had better look sharp and book his room in plenty of time or he will never find out.

Now, after five and a half months in Australia, these and many other adventures are over. The wine list in the sharp end of a Cathay Pacific 747 brought to an end my resolve to forego alcohol for Lent – it lasted for thirty-one days – and these words are being written as steady rain is dissolving the last of the winter's snow in the depths of Gloucestershire. I have just read that Australia has beaten England by two wickets in yet another one-day international, being played this time in Sharjah in the United Arab Emirates by kind permission of Abdul Rahman Bukhatir, a cricket entrepreneur with a name to conjure with. In eight days' time I shall be flying off to spend another Greek Easter in Lindos. The wheel has come another full circle, we are all a year older and the Australians arrive in England on 30th April. Then, it will start all over again.

While I was in Rhodes another cataclysmic event descended on the game in Australia and each day more news filtered through to Zenia's newspaper shop in Lindos. The South Africans were organizing a rebel Australian team to tour South Africa the following November. Their agent provocateur in place was the former New South Wales and Australian opening batsman Bruce Francis, who is the Republic's greatest supporter, and it turned out that seven of the side to tour England had signed in spite of a contract with the Australian Cricket Board which was valid until September 1986 and forbade them to do so or at least insisted they kept themselves available at all times for Board cricket in Australia. An unlikely saviour was now found in Kerry Packer who had of course disrupted world cricket in 1977 with the foundation of World Series Cricket. Now he sprang to the defence of the Board, or maybe it was primarily to the defence of his own Channel Nine which had planned a massive coverage by satellite of the series in England. The result was that four players, Wellham, Wayne Phillips, Wood and Bennett tore up their South African contracts and rebooked their flights to England.

We may never know the inducement which decided them to do this. The other three players, Alderman, McCurdy and Rixon, were not brought back and as they refused to sign a document saying they would not go to South Africa they were replaced. The selectors turned first to Ray Phillips, Rackemann and Maguire, only to find that the last two had already signed for South Africa. Jeff Thomson was therefore called up for a last tour and the final place went to the New South Wales fast bowler David Gilbert. At the time Allan Border was worried about the disparity in payments between those four players who we are told had been given a considerable financial inducement to return to the fold and those on the basic fee of $21,000. Border threatened to pull out and Kim Hughes was placed on standby to bring the side. Border then changed his mind; why we may never know. Soon after arriving in England he had to deny a story which broke in a South African paper that he had been offered half a million dollars to captain the rebel tour.

The Australians arrived in England and gradually the names of more of those committed to South Africa began to filter through. Hogg, Dyson and Smith were former Test players who had decided to go and soon afterwards Hughes himself turned up in South Africa and said that he was going to captain the side. Graham Yallop was another to announce his involvement while in England Wessels and Ritchie were forced to deny involvement. It is another festering sore which will be with the game for some long time. Australian Prime Minister Bob Hawke has denounced those who are going saying among other things that their income tax returns will be on top of the pile. The Australian Cricket Board are suing the players who have by deciding to go to South Africa broken their contracts with the Board. The South Africans themselves are likely to sue Packer and company for inducing those who had already signed for South Africa to break their contracts and go to England. The lawyers will have a field day with massive pay cheques at the end of it all and once again cricket will be the Aunt Sally who loses. Meanwhile on with the Ashes series in England.